WASTE NOT, WANT NOT
KOSHER COOKBOOK

WASTE NOT, WANT NOT

KOSHER COOKBOOK

Creative Ways to Serve Yesterday's Meal

YAFFA FRUCHTER

KTAV Publishing

URIM PUBLICATIONS
Jerusalem • New York

Waste Not, Want Not
Kosher Cookbook
Creative Ways to Serve Yesterday's Meal
By Yaffa Fruchter
Copyright © 2019 Yaffa Fruchter

Book layout by Ariel Walden

Printed in USA
First Edition

ISBN 978-1-60280-336-7

KTAV Publishing
527 Empire Boulevard
Brooklyn, NY 11225
www.ktav.com

Urim Publications
P.O. Box 52287
Jerusalem 9152102
www.UrimPublications.com

Library of Congress Cataloging-in-Publication Data

Names: Fruchter, Yaffa, author.
Title: Waste not, want not kosher cookbook : creative ways to serve
    yesterday's meal / Yaffa Fruchter.
Description: First edition. | Brooklyn, NY : KTAV Publishing, 2019. |
    Includes index.
Identifiers: LCCN 2019008168 | ISBN 9781602803367 (hardcover : alk.
    paper)
Subjects: LCSH: Jewish cooking. | LCGFT: Cookbooks.
Classification: LCC TX724 .F784 2019 | DDC 641.5/676—dc23
LC record available at https://lccn.loc.gov/2019008168

Acknowledgments

I would like to first thank my dear friend Chana Gilboa, who said, while eating with us one day, "Yaffa, this meal is so good; you must write a cookbook!" Five years later, here we are.

Thank you to Angela and Freddy who supported me immeasurably with outstanding professional advice and gracious encouragement. They spent many hours with me making sure that I would not give up. I am lucky to have them as my friends. There aren't enough words to describe how immensely indebted I am to them.

Thanks to you this book exists.

Much gratitude to Tzvi Mauer, Michal Alatin and Pearl Friedman at Urim Publications for all their efforts in producing this cookbook.

Special personal thanks to Naomi Mauer, associate publisher of The Jewish Press whose optimistic personality was both inspiring and encouraging.

Last, but not least, I thank my husband and children who enabled me to get started, by typing my recipes. Their patience, encouragement and support cheered me on throughout this adventure. Thank you for being there for me.

↗ Clockwise from top left: *Burritos, page 68; Tastes Like Humus, page 67; Baked Garlic Challah, page 117; Chicken Meatballs, page 49.*

WASTE NOT, WANT NOT

KOSHER COOKBOOK

Contents

Introduction

My Cooking Legacy

I was born in Czechoslovakia and moved to Israel when I was just under a year old. I grew up in Israel with my parents, sister and a grandmother.

My mother and grandmother were always involved with cooking. They would start each day talking about the meal they were going to prepare. The food was prepared by the two of them, everything from scratch, fresh and nicely presented. Neither one took short cuts or ever complained about how hard it is to cook. They would make stuffed cabbage – enough for an army – and the sweet, pungent smell would linger throughout the house for days. With no freezer around, everything was shared with relatives and friends to enjoy. When the cooks decided to make phyllo dough, the whole house was literally *covered* with flour since phyllo dough has to dry on a table, each table-full yielding one roll when done. Thank goodness we have short cuts for this tedious process today!

Years later, my mother opened a restaurant which was famous for its homemade meals. My mother used to say that the best compliment she could receive from guests, was that a particular soup or dish reminded them of their mother's cooking. (The soup might have been very different from their mother's soup, but if it reminded them of their own mother's, it felt good). I remember my aged grandmother standing for hours on end frying schnitzel and then standing at the doorway smiling as she watched the happy diners enjoying her handiwork. Once people realized she was there, they would shower her with compliments, the praise lighting up her face. She lived for being able to give to others, and in her simple and loving way she taught me what is important in life.

So, as you see, I come from a legacy of life revolving around the kitchen. From early childhood I was involved with cooking, preparing and serving food for guests. The food was ready for same day consumption, with nutrition and freshness a paramount goal.

When I got married I adjusted my cooking skills to the *modern world*. I learned short cuts and the advantages of partially ready food (such as frozen phyllo dough). I reduced the amount of oil in my cooking, trying my best, however, not to compromise on freshness, nutrition, taste and variety.

Why I Wrote this Book

By choosing the subject of leftovers, I took upon myself a tall order. I am presenting you with dishes composed of ingredients commonly found in your home, a challenging endeavor. And that is why I would like to call this book a "cooking course." The explanations are as important as the recipes themselves, and once you follow the recipes, you will have the confidence to create something new on your own. This book will help you discover and appreciate the benefits of using leftovers to create tasty and healthy new dishes.

How is Eating Leftovers Good for You?

By using the leftovers that we have on hand we help the environment, develop our creativity in the kitchen, save money, and have more time to spend with our family.

Cut Back on Waste

I write this book as a mission; an antidote for the waste of food we accept without question and accountability. We give our children and others the wrong message when we throw out food. We imply that food has no value and that the money we spend on food does not count. Waste is ignored as well as the energy used by the cook in preparation of the meal, not to mention the energy spent in growing and transporting the food by farmers and others.

Yesterday I opened the refrigerator and found many small amounts of cooked foods in several containers. It is the end of the week, which means that I am cooking fresh for Shabbos. So I decided to make a *kugel* out of all the little leftovers. I had some cooked noodles, a little spinach, a little eggplant, fried onions, as well as some grilled sweet potato in garlic. I combined all these ingredients, added three eggs, a cup of flour, oil, salt, pepper and garlic powder and baked the mixture for an hour and a half at 350° F degrees. The result was a tasty success, and when the "tasters" (my children) said "Oh, it's so delicious," that was all the reward I needed.

FACT: According to an article in The Washington Post, we throw away billions of dollars' worth of food every year ("*How the U.S. manages to waste $165 billion in food each year*" by Brad Plumer, August 22, 2012)! We give our children the wrong message – that food has no value. As religious Jews, we have to undo this misconception, at least in our homes. We cannot control what's happening at parties, catering halls and the like, but we can and must control the waste of food inside our own homes. In the long run, we will appreciate and enjoy the food created from leftovers in many ways. Everybody's talking today about going "green." Using leftovers is the easiest way to do so. Going green means using and reusing our resources in order to avoid deflating naturally existing reserves for generations after us. Currently, we are using natural resources at a faster pace than nature can replace them.

The idea of conserving and reusing resources can also be applied to our food consumption. If we consider how much energy was used in the production and delivery of food to our home, we would realize the value of avoiding waste. New ways are yet to be discovered which will enable us to use leftover foods in manners we cannot predict today. For example, there are cars today that run on used vegetable oil. So if you want to go green, start in your very own kitchen.

Get Creative

This book will help you develop your own creativity in the kitchen. It is geared to both the beginner cook and the savvy chef and will give you the opportunity to use ingredients already in your refrigerator and in your pantry, and feel comfortable to produce new dishes. I want you to feel free to make up your own recipes and flexible enough and comfortable enough to adjust and adapt recipes. I hope that this book will help you develop the ability to foresee, more or less how a certain dish will turn out to be when complete. I want you to take mundane ingredients or leftover food and present the results as works of art.

Anyone can buy the ingredients for a fancy recipe (sometimes stopping in three separate stores to find all the exotic ingredients required), follow instructions, and produce pretty good results. My goal is to present some innovative means of using ingredients at hand, creating a meal with what you already have, by using leftovers without labeling them as such. In addition, I will show which ingredients can be substituted in a recipe, which ingredients are integral to the recipe, which ingredients can be added to a recipe from leftovers, and which ingredients you can eliminate and still achieve good results. For example, if you don't like caraway seeds and a recipe calls for ½ teaspoon of that spice, you can probably leave it out and still prepare a delicious dish. However, when the recipe is caraway seed soup (very Hungarian), dropping the caraway seeds will result in a tasteless soup.

I would like to use leftovers in a new way, to change texture, color, and presentation so that your family will consider the meal as new and not as boring "leftovers." In most cases, last night's supper can be presented in a new and fun way. For example, if you have leftover chicken from last night, you can use the recipe for blintzes that calls for cooked chicken.

Using leftovers does require some planning and foresight. If you have twenty chicken quarters left after a party and yours is a family of four, you'll find many ideas on how to handle this "problem." And I hope each time you will use a different approach. Your reward for the extra effort will be the priceless comment, "Oh Mommy/Daddy, it's so good!" Please don't shy away from sauces and be sure to present even small children with "fancy" foods. My experience with children is that they ate what I put on the table *repeatedly*. While beets, eggplant, and butternut squash became regular and welcome vegetables in our home, my children noticed that their friends did not eat these vegetables!

Spend More Time with Family, and Save Money

Food is a means to communicate and reach out to every member of the family with love. Through food we are able to reconnect with our creator and feel more spiritual even though food is seemingly a physical substance. Through food we teach our kids tradition; we teach how to connect to generations long gone. Our past lives on within us through the recipes and dishes left by our ancestors. The legacy of our mothers and grandmothers remains alive through the food we serve our family today. Lastly, don't forget that homemade food has a life of its own when served with love. The personal touch far outweighs any store bought alternative.

Waste Not Want Not Kosher Cookbook presents the opportunity to cook with the family, and when we learn some simple short cuts we will be able to fit home cooking into our busy lives. Once you factor in the time you drive, look for parking, get to the store, stand on line, run home, and reheat the food, you can cook your own food at home with much less stress, more satisfaction and almost the same time spent. If you feel that your life style is too hectic to accommodate your own cooked meals, use the extra money you would spend on take-out food to hire help to wash the extra dishes. Home cooking can be immensely satisfying and even more, provides the opportunity to use fresh ingredients, no preservatives and the healthiest cooking methods for preparing food.

cheese –

Feb. 3

Feb. 4

LESSON 1

FOOD
SAFETY

- Wasting food is wasting money and imagination.

- Love food, hate waste.

- The best bet for stretching your food budget – use every bit of what you buy.

Food Safety Tips

- When dealing with leftovers, the quality of the food must be determined. Any food which shows a change in color, smell, or taste must be discarded. To avoid such situations we must handle the food we plan to reuse with a good measure of care.

- Be wary of using a caterer's leftovers; you don't know when the dish was cooked, how long it was out on the counter, and what it really contains.

- Readymade food you buy from a deli or grocery should be eaten right away.

- Label and date all leftover food.

- Store in glass or plastic containers with airtight lids.

- Decide what you do with the "be creative food" as soon as it becomes a leftover.

- Be especially cautious with fish, meat and eggs.

- When in doubt, throw it out.

LESSON 2
CHICKEN SOUP

Much has been written about the goodness of chicken soup and its unique healing powers. I personally think that the main ingredient is our *Yiddishe* mother's love but that cannot be measured or proven. I will concentrate on my personal method of preparing chicken soup, which upon first glance may appear lengthy and complicated. Therefore, please read the following paragraphs and I assure you it will save time in the long run.

On a basic level, to cook chicken soup you need chicken, vegetables (carrots, onion, parsley), spices (salt, pepper, and garlic powder), and water to cover all ingredients. Cook for about an hour and presto! You have chicken soup. My chicken soup, on the other hand, is a production. I do not cook soup every week because I prepare enough for a few weeks. But once I am done, I have much more than a soup. From that soup I have the carrots and potatoes for potato salad, vegetables to serve with the main, and much more. Once you see how many short cuts this one soup can produce for other dishes, it will not be so intimidating and it will be worthwhile to try.

In my description below, I explain the role of every vegetable, since each one gives its own unique taste to the soup, but you don't have to use all of the vegetables every time you cook the soup. Of course, the more veggies you do use, the more flavorful the soup will be. You can alternate or introduce new ones each time you prepare a new batch of soup.

After putting so much effort into cooking chicken soup, you shouldn't waste one drop of it. Drain it through a sieve and the clear soup can be stored in covered containers divided according to your family size. Even the cloudy soup at the bottom of the container is used up in my house. When the soup settles, the liquid in the bottom goes into the *cholent*.

I usually cook soup in a 20-quart pot. I leave the containers of the ready soup for a day in the refrigerator. Once the fat accumulates on top I remove it and freeze the amount I am going to use for a later date. Ready, homemade soup, divided according to my family size, is a very welcoming sight on a busy *Erev* Shabbat.

Now what do we do with leftover soup after Shabbos? You can still refreeze it or you can leave it for consumption during the week. You can use it instead of water as a base for other soups, and if it is still around at the end of the week, it goes into the *cholent* used instead of water. (Where else?)

Yaffa's
Chicken Soup Recipe

Ingredients

⇨ **Water** to cover all ingredients, plus 3 Cups

⇨ **3–4 Knuckle Bones (knee bones)**
I love knuckle bones, as they give body and taste to the soup and are delicious to eat. They cook 3–4 hours. Chicken bones are messy, not so flavorful and it's hard to remove them from the soup. If you like them put them in a mesh (cheese cloth) before you place them in the pot.

⇨ **4–8 Chicken quarters** (or more as needed)

The Vegetables

All vegetables listed below should be peeled and seeded (as needed)

⇨ **1 Butternut Squash, small**
I love butternut squash. I eat it mashed or sliced.

⇨ **¼ Wedge of Cabbage**

⇨ **½ Head of Cauliflower**
Tied in mesh and cooked for a very short time.

⇨ **1–10 Carrots**
Carrots add sweetness to the soup. You can put in one or ten – it's up to you.

⇨ **2–3 Stalks Celery**
You can always add a few stalks.

⇨ **1 Celery Knob** The celery knob adds a new taste to the soup.

⇨ **1 Chayote**
This vegetable (or some may refer to it as a fruit) can be found at most fruit stands. The chayote looks like a flattened green pear and tastes like a delicious kohlrabi.

⇨ **½ of Fennel**

⇨ **4–10 Garlic Cloves**
Garlic is a very important vegetable; it adds taste to the soup. The number of cloves you use depends on the size of the pot.

⇨ **1"–2" Piece Ginger**
Ginger has a very strong taste; a little piece the size of a thumb can be felt in a large quantity of soup. I use it on occasion.

⇨ **1 Jicama**
This vegetable is a welcome newcomer in my kitchen and I hope it will be in yours too. It tastes like a sweet turnip and looks like a light brown turnip. You can eat it raw, cooked, or grated into a salad.

⇨ **1 Kohlrabi**
This is a great addition to the soup; everybody likes it plain, cooked, or added to other dishes.

⇨ **1 Onion**
I usually use one onion and discard it when the soup is ready. (If you have other ways to use the cooked onion, I'll be happy to hear from you.)

⇨ **1 Bunch Parsley Greens**
Parsley is a great vegetable; one bunch can give a very good taste to the soup and it is delicious and healthful to eat cooked. When you

reheat soup you can always add a fresh bunch – it gives a fresh smell and taste to the soup. Parsley can be placed in a removable mesh bag and is added to the pot of soup during the last 10 minutes of cooking.

⇨ **2 – 3 Parsnip Roots**
The parsnip is a delicious vegetable that looks like a white carrot.

⇨ **1 Potato**
Potato adds very little taste to the soup itself. It can be used in potato salad or other dishes, so you saved yourself washing an extra pot. Just keep in mind that the potato cooks faster than most vegetables in the soup. It will be better to use a mesh bag for easy removal.

⇨ **¼ of Rutabaga**

⇨ **1 Sweet Potato**
This is a great vegetable for the soup. It adds lots of sweetness and it is delicious to eat as a side dish. It needs a very short cooking time.

⇨ **1–2 Zucchini**
This is a great vegetable. You can peel it or leave it unpeeled. Zucchini needs a very short cooking time.

⇨ **Salt, pepper, garlic powder, very little paprika**
Can be added for taste

⇨ **(Chicken Soup Powder Mix)**
This one comes in parenthesis because I used to use it a lot in almost every dish I cooked, but now I try to avoid the MSG and processed foods, and I discovered that it is not missed.

Any combination of the above vegetables can be used in a chicken soup, the minimum being carrots, onion, garlic, and parsley. Other vegetables not mentioned above, such as green beans, broccoli, cauliflower, or asparagus can be added for a short time into the soup by putting them into a mesh bag and removing them when they are ready.

Directions

a.   Put bones, chicken, and any other meat you would like (I add all the meats I am going to use that Shabbos, (i.e., the cholent meat and the roast) into your largest pot, cover with water, and bring to a boil. Immediately remove from heat, and pour liquid out into the sink. Rinse the meat, chicken and the pot, return the meats you are going to use for the soup (i.e., only the chicken and the bones) to the pot, cover with water plus 2 to 3 additional cups of water, and return to the heat.*

b.   Add the vegetables in batches (so that there is room in the pot), starting with the root vegetables, which take the longest to cook. The root vegetables include carrots, celery knob, celery, chayote, fennel, garlic, ginger, jicama, kohlrabi, onions, parsnip, potato, rutabaga, and sweet potato. Cook until tender and remove. Soft vegetables like cabbage, cauliflower, kohlrabi, and zucchini, need only about 15 minutes of cooking in the soup.

   You *must* remove the vegetables and chicken as they become ready (so they can be used in other recipes). The bones remain in the pot of soup for the full cooking time.

c.   Remove the chicken quarters when they have cooked for about 30 minutes.

d.   Last, add the parsley greens.

e.   *For a clear soup*, once the soup comes to a boil, adjust the fire to a low simmer, and continue to cook for three to four hours.

f.   Add spices once the soup comes to a boil. Taste the soup towards the end of the cooking time and adjust seasoning.

---

*   I would like to mention that this is actually a short-cut compared to what my mother used to do. She would designate a *whole* day for cleaning the chickens. I simply use this method of boiling the water and rinsing the meat and the chicken. If I see pinfeathers or fat, I simply remove them and return the chicken and/or meat back into the pot.

Optional: When serving, many people place a piece of zucchini, carrots or butternut squash into their individual bowls of chicken soup along with noodles.

 Tip: A few pieces of cut up chicken can enrich any soup.

 Tip: Use a large circular slotted spoon to remove the vegetables from the soup as they become done.

Although this method may sound complicated, the reward is the knowledge that when you know how to cook a good chicken soup you can cook anything. And as a bonus you have all these cooked veggies to create many new variations, not to mention the large quantity of soup available.

Reusing Vegetables from the Soup 11 Different Ways

By using the vegetables from the soup for other dishes you benefit from them twice. First the vegetables release taste and nutrients into the soup and now you have a quick fix for a side dish.

Most cooked vegetables can be added in small amounts to hamburgers, meat balls, meat loaf, cholent or to other cooked leftover vegetables; pasta, rice, orzo, quinoa or the like.

1. Bubby's Vegetable Patties
2. Butternut Squash Soup
3. Cubed Vegetable Soup
4. Knob Celery
5. Kohlrabi
6. Mashed Butternut Squash
7. Moroccan Style Carrots
8. *Tsimmes*
9. Vegetable kugel
10. Vegetable Loaf
11. Zucchini with Fried Onions

BUBBY'S VEGETABLE PATTIES

A simple yet tasty dish to "mask" your chicken soup vegetables.

a. Add 1 egg and 2 Tbsp. of flour per cup of vegetables.

b. Form balls, which can also be flattened with the palm of your hand.

c. Fry in oil, or bake for half an hour at 350°F, or until heated through.

BUTTERNUT SQUASH SOUP

Ingredients
1 Butternut squash, peeled, seeded and cut into large chunks
Soup broth, for cooking
Water, enough to cover vegetables, plus 2–3 Cups
Seasoning, to taste

Directions
a. Add butternut squash chunks to soup to be cooked.
b. Remove when soft, mash well, and add some water.
c. Reheat, add seasoning and serve as a "new" soup.
⇨ *Variation*: Add about 1 cup of white roux (see below in Main Courses), mixing well. The roux will give body to the soup.

CUBED VEGETABLE SOUP

Ingredients

2 Cups Assorted vegetables, cooked
Water or soup, enough to cover
    vegetables, plus
2–3 Cups Seasoning, to taste

Directions

a. Cut up the vegetables into cubes
and return to the chicken soup for
a *fleishig* (meat) vegetable soup.
Or use water instead, adjust the
seasoning, cook for about a half
an hour and serve.

➯ *Variation 1*: Mash some of the
cooked vegetables in a pot, cover
with water, and season to taste.
Bring to a boil and you have a new
soup.

➯ *Variation 2*: Mash all ingredients
(with or without chicken) using
an immersion blender to make a
pureed vegetable soup.

➯ *Variation 3*: Add about 1 cup of
white roux (see below in Main
Courses), mixing well. The roux
will give body to the soup.

Botamochy/Shutterstock.com

KNOB CELERY

Cubed celery knob is a delicious alternative to traditional potato salad.

Ingredients
1 Celery Knob, cooked and cubed
3 Tbsp. Mayonnaise
10 Olives, sliced
½ Onion, chopped
4 Carrots, cooked and cubed
Seasoning, to taste

Directions
a. Combine all ingredients. Adjust seasoning.

⇨ *Variation*: Add 2–3 tablespoons cut up deli.

KOHLRABI

A delicious side dish served hot or at room temperature.

Ingredients
2 Kohlrabi, cut julienne style
½ Cup Onions, fried
Seasoning, to taste

Directions
a. Combine all. Adjust seasoning. You can also mix in other cooked vegetables.
The possibilities of "mix and match" are endless.

MASHED OR CUBED BUTTER-NUT SQUASH

I like this dish very much and it is ready in no time.

Ingredients
1 Cooked butternut squash, seeded, peeled and mashed
1 Cup Onions, chopped and fried (optional) in 2–3 tablespoons of oil
Seasoning to taste

Directions
a. Mix mashed squash with fried onions (optional) and seasoning. Serve warm or at room temperature.

⇨ *Variation*: Cube the squash, sand mix with the fried onions. Serve warm or at room temperature.

Paul Horwitz/Shutterstock.com

MOROCCAN STYLE CARROTS

Ingredients
5–6 Carrots, cooked and sliced
Water or clear chicken soup to
  cover vegetables
1 tsp Cumin
Salt, pepper, and crushed garlic, to
  taste

Directions
a. Cook for ½ an hour mixing occasionally. Be careful not to mash the carrots. Taste and adjust seasoning. Serve.

TSIMMES

Ingredients
4 Carrots, cooked
4–5 Prunes (optional)
2 Tbsp. Sugar
Pinch Salt
2 Tbsp. Honey

Directions
a. Slice carrots and put in a pot.

b. Add rest of ingredients.

c. Cook on low flame for about 10 minutes, mixing occasionally.

d. Can be served warm or at room temperature.

Optional: Add dates or dried apricots.

VEGETABLE KUGEL

A delicious dish.

Ingredients

6 Cups Mashed Vegetables
6 Eggs
½ Cup Oil
5 Tbsp. Flour
Salt, pepper and garlic powder, to taste

Directions

a. Mash the vegetables in a mixing bowl.

b. Add eggs, flour, salt, pepper, garlic, and oil.

c. Pour into a 9" × 13" baking pan, bake at 350° F for about an hour until golden.

✓ *Tip*: Celery should be cut into small slices before adding to the mixture.

⤵ *Variation*: Add some boneless chicken or meat pieces left from slicing a roast.

VEGETABLE LOAF

Ingredients
1 Cup Cooked vegetables
1 Egg
2 Tbsp. Flour
Seasoning, to taste

Directions
a. Mash cooked vegetables from the soup like potato, carrots, butternut squash or any of the root vegetables.
b. You may add some leftover crumbled hamburgers or cut up chicken cutlets.
c. Mix well with all ingredients.
d. Form a loaf and bake on an oiled cookie sheet for an hour at 350° F.
e. Serve hot.

➪ *Variation*: Pour 1 cup of tomato sauce or one of the sauces described later in Main Courses, on top of the loaf before baking. (My personal favorite is mushroom sauce for this dish.)

Lucie Peclova/Shutterstock.com

✓ *Tip*: This recipe can be doubled or tripled.

ZUCCHINI WITH FRIED ONIONS

Ingredients
1 Cup Zucchini, cooked in soup for a very short time.
(Make sure it is immersed in the liquid while cooking.)
2 Tbsp. Onions, fried
Seasoning, to taste

Directions
a. Remove zucchini from soup when zucchini is almost soft. Cube or cut into thick slices.
b. Add fried onions and seasoning to taste. Mix well.
c. Serve warm.

LESSON 3
CHICKEN AND TURKEY

"Chicken in Sweet Sauce," page 58.

After Shabbos, or after a big party, you have to evaluate how much food is left over and how many family meals can be prepared from it. This reorganization must be done as soon as possible. You cannot leave leftover chicken uncovered in the back of your refrigerator and at the end of the week decide, "Oh, maybe I should freeze some of these leftovers."

As soon as the food becomes "leftover" you have to decide its "fate" in order to achieve best results. If you have one drumstick left over, you can eat it cold or reheated the next day, or you can get a little more creative. You can strip the chicken from the bone, cut it into small pieces, and add it to a vegetable soup or mix it with one of the cooked vegetables you will serve the next day, for example, into a Letcho or Ratatouille. Even a fresh salad can handle a few pieces of chicken, as well as a kugel. You can decide to add it to the container with another lone drumstick you placed in the freezer last week. Just make sure it is covered properly and labeled with the date.

The fun begins when you have a larger amount and you can present the chicken in many creative ways. The original form of the chicken will not be recognized, but rather, will be fully appreciated in its new transformation (you can achieve this when the word *leftovers* is never mentioned). The best way is to divide the chicken into meal-size portions and freeze covered in airtight containers labeled with the date.

I focus on chicken because it is so popular, but we can use the same methods for almost any other meat. The most important detail about leftover chicken or meat is to remember that it has already been cooked and served, and a certain amount of time has passed since it was called *fresh*. So we have to rehydrate it, change its looks, and, many times, hide it in other foods such as dough, eggs, mayonnaise, or sauce. That doesn't mean the food is bad or should be discarded; it means that it needs help and we are here for the rescue. In the long run, you will save time and energy when you use leftovers, while stretching your food dollar at the same time. You will also enjoy the satisfaction of having tried new and creative ways to serve it differently. Another plus is the fact that you went out on a limb, to cook something special for your family which will pay off big time.

TIPS for schnitzel (chicken cutlets):

✓ Use whole wheat flour – nobody will know the difference.

✓ Shake off excess flour and bread crumbs in order to make sure the crust doesn't come off while frying.

✓ After preparing the schnitzel, fry only the ones you'll use at that meal. The rest of the cutlets with the bread crumbs on, can be stored covered in the refrigerator for one or two days.

✓ Breaded cutlets can be piled up on a plate with paper towels separating the layers. (I just discovered recently that the paper towels are better than silver foil or plastic sheets because they absorb some moisture and it is easier to separate and fry on a later date, no more than 2 days) The reason is that the Schnitzel is best freshly fried. You can re-dip them in egg wash, before frying.

Here is a list of 31 dishes that use leftover chicken, broken down into categories. (Recipes follow.)

I. Soup and Accompaniments

1. Chicken Veggie Soup
2. Cream of Chicken Soup
3. *Griven*
4. *Kreplach*

II. Salads, Appetizers and Side Dishes

1. *Blintzes*
2. *Bourekas*
3. Chicken *Kugel*

4. Chicken Meatballs
5. Chicken in Phyllo or Pastry Dough
6. Chicken Salad A
7. Chicken or Turkey Salad B
8. Chicken Wraps
9. *Falche* fish
10. Sushi

III. Main Courses

1. Casserole
2. Chicken Chinese Style
3. Chicken Frittata
4. Chicken in Sauces
5. Chicken Patties
6. Chicken Pie
7. Chicken with Biscuit on Top
8. Chicken with Fried Onions
9. Chicken with Rice
10. *Cholent*
11. Cubed Chicken with Vegetables
12. *Fleishig* (meat/chicken) pizza
13. Jerusalem Mix
14. "Kentucky" Fried Chicken (Schnitzel)
15. Mixed Chicken with Letcho
16. Mixed Chicken with Potatoes
17. Warm Turkey Dinner

LESSON 3, PART I

SOUP AND ACCOMPANIMENTS

CHICKEN VEGGIE SOUP

a. Cut cooked vegetables you have at hand (butternut squash, carrots, sweet potatoes, etc.)

b. Cover with water or chicken soup.

c. Add cut cooked chicken, season to taste, and cook for 30 minutes.

d. Serve hot.

⇨ *Variation*: you can mash some of the vegetables before serving with a potato masher or, after turning off the fire, use an emersion blender to puree the soup.

CREAM OF CHICKEN SOUP

a. Process cooked chicken removed from 3–4 chicken quarters, or a pound of cooked meat in a food processor, leaving 2–3 Tbsp. cut into small pieces.

b. Make a basic roux in a pot (see Chicken in Sauces in Lesson 3, Section III, for directions).

c. Add 2 quarts of cold chicken soup or water.

d. Bring to a boil, add mashed chicken and pieces, or leave pieces for garnish before serving.

e. Season. Simmer for about 30 minutes on low, mixing occasionally. Serve hot.

Optional: Garnish with dill or parsley.

GRIVEN

This is a delicacy known in Eastern Europe. It's very oily even though the oil is removed while cooking. You can use this for special occasions or for people who remember the taste of the olden days. It is a great example for not throwing anything out.

a. Save the skins of cooked chicken which were removed from other recipes, and store in the freezer.

b. When you have about 3–4 cups full, defrost and place in a frying pan, letting it cook for a while (with nothing added), removing and discarding the melting fat with a spoon once in a while.

c. When it looks crispy all over, (make sure not to burn the skin and not to remove from fire before it's crispy), sprinkle a few drops of water on top and remove the crisped skin right away into a sieve.

d. Enjoy. Best served fresh.

KREPLACH

Ingredients
(for 1 cup of filling, or 10–15 *kreplach*)

Store bought frozen puff pastry squares or roll out dough*
2 Chicken quarters, cooked
2 Large Onions, chopped and fried
Salt & Pepper to taste

Directions

a. Use store bought frozen dough squares. (If not precut, roll out and cut into 2" × 2" squares.)

b. Fill with chicken pieces mixed with fried onions, salt and pepper. Each *kreplach* needs only about a teaspoon of filling.

c. Form triangles.

d. Close the edges tightly and lay them on a floured surface, not touching each other. Cook in boiling water with a little salt for about 15 minutes. Strain and arrange in a single layer in a greased 9" × 13" pan.

e. Lay a piece of silver foil on top, sprayed with oil and repeat. Cover and keep in fridge.

f. For immediate use, rewarm in clear, hot soup.

g. Serves 2–3 *kreplach* per person.

h. Can be stored in freezer for up to 3 months.

- -

* To prepare your own dough:

2 Cups Flour
1 Egg
1 tsp. Salt
2 Tbsp. Oil
2 Tbsp. Water

Mix all ingredients. Let rest for half an hour. Divide dough into 4 equal parts. Roll out each part very thinly. Cut 2" × 2" squares. Fill each square with about 1 teaspoon of chicken mixture. Fold over forming a triangle. Press edges together very firmly. Proceed as above.

⇨ *Variation*: Fry in oil one layer at a time.

LESSON 3, PART II

SALADS,
APPETIZERS
& SIDE DISHES

BLINTZES

This is a delicious dish. Not only is it far from looking like leftovers but once you try it you will cook extra chicken in order to have enough for this dish. There are no leftovers in my house from this delicacy.

Blintzes

4 Cups Water
6 Eggs
2 Tbsp. Oil
Pinch Salt
4 Cups Flour
Salt & Pepper
Oil to coat pan when frying

Directions

a. Add all ingredients in a large bowl, starting with the flour.
b. Mix well with a metal whisk. The consistency should feel like buttermilk.
c. Pour a ladleful into a heated and greased frying pan, turning the pan around and around until the batter thinly coats the pan. Turn over when the surface looks dry.
d. Fry the other side for a minute, and slide the blintz onto a plate. You can pile them one on top of the other.

Yields about 3 dozen blintzes

✓ **Tip** – To use as little oil as possible, pour oil into a small bowl, and use a paper towel to brush the pan in between blintzes.

✓ **Tip** – For Passover you can use the same batter, substituting potato starch for flour.

✓ **Tip** – On Passover you can use these blintzes as noodles for the soup by slicing them into thin strips.

Filling

6 Chicken quarters, preferably bottoms, stripped off the bone and cut into very small pieces (You can process it in the food processor but it won't be as good as cut by hand)
2 Cups Fried onions, drained
Salt, pepper, & garlic powder, to taste

Directions

a. Mix all ingredients.

b. Put about 2–4 Tbsp. (depending on the size of the blintz) of the mixture on each blintz next to one edge, fold over both sides and roll firmly to the other edge.

c. Arrange one next to the other in a 9" × 13" pan and pour sauce over it.

d. At this point you can freeze them covered and labeled.

Sauce

4 Tbsp. Flour
6 Tbsp. Oil
4 Tbsp. Osem mushroom soup mix
Salt, pepper, & garlic powder to taste
1 Quart Cold water

Directions

a. Before starting, prepare a quart jar of cold water next to the stove.

b. Mix the first 3 ingredients very well in a pot. Add spices, turn on heat and keep mixing, until mixture turns light brown. Make sure it's not too dark. If you burn it, start all over again.

c. Adjust seasoning.

d. Pour the cold water at once into the hot mixture. Keep mixing until all water is incorporated.

e. Continue cooking, mixing continuously until thick sauce forms.

f. Cover pot if you are not planning to use it right away. If you use this method you will never have lumps.

g. Pour sauce onto rolled up blintzes and reheat, covered, in oven at 250° F until ready to use. Or freeze for a future use.

BOUREKAS

CHICKEN *KUGEL*

Directions

a. Use small frozen bourekas squares or flaky dough.

b. Fill with the chicken mixture presented in the blintze recipe above.

c. Arrange on a sprayed cookie sheet. You can freeze this batch at this point.

d. Bake for 30 minutes at 350° F.

Variations:

⇨ Use Mashed Potatoes as a filling. (See recipe in the Vegetable Section of Lesson 6.)

⇨ Mix in a cupful of other cooked root vegetables such as carrots or chayote as optional fillings as well.

Ingredients

4 Cups Cooked chicken
2 Cups Cooked vegetable of choice (carrots, potatoes, zucchini, etc.)
6 Eggs
1 Cup Flour
2 Tbsp. Oil
Salt, pepper, garlic powder to taste

Directions

Mix all ingredients and pour into an oiled 9" × 13" pan.
Bake for an hour on 375°F.

⇨ *Variation*: Before baking sprinkle the top of the *kugel* with 4 Tbsp. bread crumbs mixed with 2 Tbsp. oil.

CHICKEN MEATBALLS

Ingredients
1 Egg
1 Cup Cooked chicken, skin and bones removed
1 Tbsp. Fried onions
4 Tbsp. Water
4 Tbsp. Flour or bread crumbs
Salt, pepper and garlic to taste
2 Tbsp. Tomato sauce for meatball mixture
1–2 Cans Tomato sauce, enough to cover meatballs before baking.
Seasonings to taste

Directions
a. Pulse chicken in food processor to the size of peas.
b. Add egg.
c. Add fried onions, water and 2 Tbsp. tomato sauce.
d. Add flour or bread crumbs.
e. Add salt, pepper and garlic. Mix well.
f. Make small balls and roll them very tightly in your hands. Lay them in a baking pan.
g. Cover with tomato sauce.
h. Sprinkle with additional seasonings on top.
i. Bake for a half hour on 350° F.

⇨ *Variation 1*: Use any of the sauces from Lesson 3, Section III Main Courses, instead of tomato sauce.

⇨ *Variation 2*: Omit the tomato sauce and drop the balls into boiling water with 1 Tbsp. of salt, in a large pot. Cook for ½ an hour, remove balls, drain. Serve hot.

CHICKEN IN PHYLLO DOUGH OR PASTRY DOUGH

Filling (for phyllo dough, pastry dough, or bourekas)

2 Cups Cooked chicken, turkey or meat cut into small pieces (no bones)
(I like the chicken cut by hand but you can pulse it in the food processor. It will have a slightly different texture when using the machine.)
1–2 Eggs
Leftover Cooked veggies (if you have) like potatoes, carrots, etc., cubed (optional)
4 Tbsp. Fried onions
½ Cup Flour
Salt & pepper
2–3 Cloves Crushed Garlic
2–3 Tbsp. Oil
Salt, pepper, and garlic powder to taste

Directions

a. Mix all ingredients in a bowl.

For phyllo dough

i. Brush each leaf with oil or spray.
ii. Put 4 leaves into cupcake shaped pan or ramekins.
iii. Fill with the chicken mixture and bake at 350° F for about 30 minutes.
iv. Can be served hot or at room temperature.

For chicken in dough use frozen pastry dough

i. Roll out dough half inch thick
ii. Fill one side with the chicken mixture roll up jelly roll fashion.
iii. Brush with egg wash and bake for an hour at 350° F.

CHICKEN SALAD A

Ingredients

4 Quarters Chicken or meat, cooked and stripped off the bones.
½ Onion, chopped
½ Cup Cooked carrots, sliced or cubed
4 Pickles, cubed or thinly sliced
4 Tbsp. Mayonnaise
Salt, pepper, and garlic powder, to taste
4 Tbsp. Pickle juice or vinegar
1 Tbsp. Sugar (optional)
Parsley, for decoration and/or chopped up and added to the salad

Directions

a. Cut the chicken or meat into small cubes, and put in a large bowl. (You can save the skin for *Griven*. See *recipe in Lesson 3*).
b. Add carrots, onion, and pickles to chicken.
c. Add mayonnaise, pickle juice and seasoning. Mix well.
d. Serve decorated with parsley and carrot slices on the smoothed top.

⇨ *Variation*: Add ½ cup peas and or ½ cup corn.

CHICKEN OR TURKEY SALAD B

Ingredients

3 Cups Cooked chicken or turkey, boned and cubed
⅔ Cups Mayonnaise
2 Tbsp. Lemon juice
Salt and pepper to taste
1 ½ Cups Raisins or dried cranberries
3 Stalks Celery, chopped thinly
½ Cup Nuts and/or sunflower seeds, chopped

Directions

a. Mix mayonnaise, salt and lemon juice.
b. In large bowl, mix meat, raisins and celery.
c. Pour dressing over cooked meat.
d. Chill for about an hour.
e. Before serving, mix with nuts and garnish with parsley leaves.

A. Zhuravleva/Shutterstock.com

CHICKEN WRAPS

a. Use same mixture as above for the blintz filling.
b. Smear a wrap with mayonnaise and mustard.
c. Add the filling and any green leaves on top of the mixture.
d. Roll up. Warm in a frying pan on both sides.
e. Serve hot with some salsa sauce.

emrahphoto/Shutterstock.com

SUSHI

Use tiny pieces of meat or cold cuts instead of fish when you prepare sushi.

Enlightened Media/Shutterstock.com

FALCHE FISH

Falche fish means "mock" fish. My mother used to do this when there was no fish at the market. This is a delicious dish with a bad name. I would prepare this any time. For best results, use a meat grinder and not a food processor.

Salvomassara/Shutterstock.com

Ingredients
1 Cup Chicken cutlet, cooked (leftover) and ground
1 Egg
2 Tbsp. Matzo meal
2 tsp. Salt
2 tsp. Sugar

Directions
a. Mix all ingredients, with wet hands and form elongated balls.
b. Drop them one by one into a large pot of salted boiling water. Simmer for about 20 minutes. Remove from pot with a large slotted spoon and drain.
c. Serve hot or cold, as is or with tomato sauce. Enjoy.

LESSON 3, PART III

MAIN COURSES

1 CASSEROLE

2 CHICKEN CHINESE STYLE

3 CHICKEN FRITTATA

4 CHICKEN IN SAUCES

5 CHICKEN PATTIES

6 CHICKEN PIE

7 CHICKEN WITH BISCUIT ON TOP

8 CHICKEN WITH FRIED ONIONS

9 CHICKEN WITH RICE

10 *CHOLENT*

11 CUBED CHICKEN WITH VEGETABLES

12 *FLEISHIG* (MEAT/CHICKEN) PIZZA

13 JERUSALEM MIX

14 "KENTUCKY" FRIED CHICKEN (SCHNITZEL)

15 MIXED CHICKEN WITH LETCHO

16 MIXED CHICKEN WITH POTATOES

17 WARM TURKEY DINNER

CASSEROLE

This is an easy way to refresh what you have in a very short time and requires little effort.

Ingredients

2½ Cups Roux (See Chicken in *Sauces* later in this section, for basic roux directions)
1 Cup Chicken, sliced or shredded
½ Cup Pearl onions or fried onions
1 Cup Cooked carrots, sliced
1 Cup Cooked asparagus or green beans, cut into 1-inch pieces
½ Cup Bread crumbs
1 Tbsp. Oil plus oil to grease bottom of dish

Directions

a. In a greased casserole dish pour half of the roux and arrange ½ of chicken on top.

b. Arrange half of each vegetable one on top of the other in the dish. Repeat.

c. Mix bread crumbs with oil, pour on top of the vegetables.

d. Bake at 400° F about 45 minutes. *Yields 4 servings.*

CHICKEN CHINESE STYLE

ui7711/Shutterstock.com

a. Mix de-boned pieces of chicken with a package of frozen Chinese vegetable mix.
b. Warm in frying pan.
c. Add salt, pepper, garlic and 3 Tablespoons of soy sauce.

Optional: Add cashews when ready to serve.

CHICKEN FRITTATA

Ingredients
6 Eggs
4 Tbsp. Flour
Salt, Pepper
Fried onions
½ Cup each Peas and cooked
    carrots
1 Cup Chicken pieces, cooked and
    cut small
Fresh smashed garlic or garlic
    powder
1 Tbsp. Parsley flakes

Directions
a. Mix eggs in a bowl.
b. Add rest of ingredients.
c. Bake at 350° F in an oiled, round dish for 1 hour or until frittata is firm on top.

Nataliya Arzamasova/Shutterstock.com

CHICKEN IN SAUCES

A base for the tomato, garlic and mushroom sauces is a *roux*.* These three sauces are variations of a basic roux. The Sweet Sauce is an additional option to enjoy with your leftover chicken.

The cooked chicken can be cut in quarters or eighths.

Warm the chicken in a 350° F oven for about 10 minutes.

Pour one of the following sauces over the chicken, enough to generously coat each portion, and return to oven for another 10 minutes.

Nobody will fault you for serving leftovers as this is delicious in its own right.

*Basic *roux* is prepared in the following manner: Cook flour and oil together over low heat until light brown. Quickly add a large amount of water and stir until desired thickness is achieved, mixing constantly. Add salt, garlic powder and black pepper to taste.

▶ Tomato Sauce

This sauce does not look like tomato sauce from a can. It is lighter in color, creamier, and full of flavor.

Ingredients
4 Tbsp. Flour
4 Tbsp. Oil
4 Tbsp. Ketchup
Salt, pepper, and garlic powder to taste
1 Tbsp. Sugar
1 Quart Water

Directions
a. Cook flour and oil together, mixing occasionally.
b. Once it's light brown, add ketchup, and then all the water at once, mixing vigorously until desired thickness is achieved.
c. Add seasonings. Taste, correct seasoning.

Foodio/Shutterstock.co

▶ Garlic Sauce

This is a great sauce and I use it in many dishes. When you prepare it, the aroma of the garlic permeates through the house.

Same as Tomato Sauce but omit the ketchup, and add 3 tsp. crushed garlic in the beginning of the process.

▶ Sweet Sauce

Ingredients
1 Cup Apricot sauce *or*
½ Cup Chicken soup mixed with
½ Cup Crushed pineapple and
2 Tbsp. Sugar

info/Shutterstock.com

▶ Mushroom Sauce

Add 2 Tbsp. of mushroom soup mix to the garlic sauce.

hlphoto/Shutterstock.com

CHICKEN PATTIES

Directions
a. Use chicken mixture from chicken filling for dough. (See recipe above, *Chicken in Phyllo Dough.*)
b. Form flatted balls.
c. Fry in oil on both sides.
d. Remove to plate lined with a paper towel.
e. Serve hot.

Timolina/Shutterstock.com

CHICKEN PIE

A great way to use leftover chicken or any other meat. Nobody will know that it is leftovers.

Ingredients

2 Cups Chicken cut up
½ - 1 Cup Fried onions, drained
3 Tomatoes, chopped
Salt, pepper, and garlic powder, to taste
½ Green pepper, cut small
½ Cup Frozen peas
2 Tbsp. Fresh parsley, chopped
2 Frozen pie shell, defrosted and baked for 10 minutes.
3 Eggs

Directions

a. Mix onions, salt, pepper, and tomatoes, and cook in a pot for about 5 minutes, mixing occasionally.
b. Add rest of ingredients besides eggs. Cook 1 minute. Let cool a bit.
c. Mix the eggs in a bowl and add to the mixture while mixing fast.
d. Pour into pie crust.
e. Bake at 400° F for about 30 minutes. *Yields 4 servings.*

CHICKEN WITH BISCUIT ON TOP

Ingredients for Filling

2 Cups Cooked chicken, cubed
½ Cup Fried onions, drained
2 Green peppers, cut small
1 Can Sliced mushrooms
2 Tbsp. Corn starch
1–½ Cups Water
Salt & Pepper To taste

Directions

a. Heat all vegetables and chicken in a well-oiled pan. Cook 1 minute.
b. Add cornstarch and stir.
c. Add water and bring to a boil.
d. Transfer to a baking dish.

Ingredients for Biscuit

2 Cups Flour
1 tsp. Salt
2-½ tsp. Baking soda
⅓ Cup Margarine
⅔ Cup Water

Directions

a. Sift first 3 ingredients and put in food processor.
b. Add margarine cut into pieces. Process with metal knife attachment until small clumps form. Add water until dough is soft but not sticky.

c. Knead about 10 minutes.

d. Roll dough out on a floured board or surface to a thickness of one inch and cut rounds with a cup or a cookie cutter.

e. Place on top of chicken.

f. Bake 15 minutes.
   Yields 4 servings.

CHICKEN WITH FRIED ONIONS

For a fast supper, warm up cooked cubed chicken with fried onions. Season and serve.

CHICKEN WITH RICE

Directions

a. Left over chicken cut into eighths (with or without bone) or cubed. Set aside.

b. Cook rice as directed, adding an extra ½ to 1 cup water (for extra moist rice).

c. Add the chicken for the last 10 minutes of cooking time or until chicken is heated through.

Optional: Add cut up fried egg and vegetables.

CHOLENT

Add leftover boneless chicken or meat to your *cholent*.

CUBED CHICKEN WITH VEGETABLES

Cubed chicken can be mixed with sliced mushrooms, peas, cooked carrots slices, canned or fresh corn, or any other leftover cooked vegetables, salt, pepper and garlic powder.

Make sure you do not prepare more than your family eats in one meal or you will be stuck with leftovers of leftovers!

Reheat. Mix for five minutes. Ready!

FLEISHIG (MEAT/CHICKEN) PIZZA

Ingredients

1 package Pizza dough (parev)
½ Cup Tomato sauce
2–3 Cloves Garlic, chopped
2 Fresh leaves Basil, chopped
2 Quarters Boneless pieces of chicken *or*
4–5 Slices Cold cuts
1 Cup Fried onions
½ Cup White sauce (roux)

Directions

a. Roll out a pizza (*parev*) dough.
b. Spread tomato sauce evenly on dough.
c. Sprinkle garlic and basil on top.
d. Place slices of cold cuts or boneless pieces of chicken evenly over sauce.
e. Add fried onions and a white sauce made out of roux (see Chicken in Sauces in lesson 3, Section III above), drizzled on top.
f. Bake for 30 minutes at 400° F.

⇨ *Variation*: Instead of White sauce, try Garlic or Mushroom Sauce (see *Chicken in Sauces in Lesson 3, Section III above, or use chopped canned mushrooms*). Add 3–4 drops of yellow food coloring to the sauce and pour over pizza. Proceed with step c above.

JERUSALEM MIX

Ingredients

2 Cups Cooked chicken, liver, meat, and/or cold cuts
1 Cup Fried onions
1 Tbsp. Shawarma spice
Salt, pepper and garlic powder to taste

Directions

a. Cut chicken/liver/meat/cold cuts into small pieces.
b. Add the fried onions, shawarma spice and seasonings.
c. Heat and serve immediately.

"KENTUCKY" FRIED CHICKEN (SCHNITZEL)

Ingredients

4 Chicken quarters or 8 eighths, (Skin can be removed if desired.)
1 Cup Flour
2 Eggs mixed with a few drops of water
1 Cup Bread crumbs*

Directions

a. Prepare three bowls. One for flour, another for eggs mixed with a few drops of water, and a third plate for bread crumbs.

b. Dip each portion of chicken in flour, then egg and last, bread crumbs.

c. Two ways to proceed:

(i) Arrange dipped and coated chicken pieces on a greased baking sheet. Drizzle chicken lightly with oil. Bake for a half hour in the oven on 350°F.

OR

ii. Fry each dipped and coated chicken piece in hot oil, enough to generously cover bottom of frying pan. Turn once.

*Dried challah processed in food processor can be used for the bread crumbs.

Warning: The second method requires caution. The cooked chicken contains small droplets of water. These droplets heat slowly in the frying process and can explode in the hot oil. It is true this method is delicious but be very, very careful.

MIXED CHICKEN WITH LETCHO

MIXED CHICKEN WITH POTATOES

Ingredients

- 2 Cups Cooked Chicken or meat, cut into bite sized pieces
- 4 Tbsp. Oil
- 4 Onions, chopped
- 4 Carrots, grated
- 4 Peppers, in a variety of colors, cubed
- 4 Tomatoes, chopped
- 1 Cup Tomato sauce
- 2 Tbsp. Sugar (optional)
- Salt, Pepper, Garlic to taste

Directions

a. Fry onions in oil until light brown. Add carrots and peppers. Continue frying for 10–15 minutes, mixing occasionally.

b. Add tomatoes, tomato sauce, sugar (optional), salt, pepper and garlic and continue to cook on low flame for 10 minutes.

c. Add bite sized cut chicken about 1:1 ratio with the letcho.

d. This letcho can be mixed into pasta or rice for an easy, new side dish.

Directions

a. If you cooked potatoes in the soup or you have some from a previous meal, add some leftover chicken on or off the bone to some cubed potatoes.

b. Add fried onions.

c. Add salt and pepper to taste. Presto! You have a new side dish.

⇨ *Variation*: Use mashed potatoes instead of cooked potatoes, and mix with chicken or other cooked meat (*without* bones), fried onions, salt and pepper to taste.

Fanfo/Shutterstock.com

Timolina/Shutterstock.com

WARM TURKEY DINNER

Ingredients

- 2 tsp. Canola oil
- 2 tsp. Each: Paprika, ground cumin (optional), turmeric (optional)
- 1 tsp. Ginger
- 1 large Onion, chopped
- 2 tsp. Garlic, minced
- ½ Cup Chicken soup
- 1 Cup *Parev* milk
- 4 Cups Cooked turkey or chicken cubed
- 1½ Cups Frozen peas, defrosted

Directions

a. Heat oil and add spices. Cook for a few minutes.

b. Add onions and garlic. Cook an additional few minutes.

c. Add broth and *parev* milk. Simmer, for about seven minutes, stirring occasionally.

d. Add turkey and peas, heat through.

e. Serve immediately.

Kiian Oksana/Shutterstock.com

"Bean Soup," page 67.

LESSON 4
CHOLENT, RICE AND PASTA

LESSON 4, PART 1

CHOLENT

What are we going to do with that delicious and welcoming cholent *once Shabbat is over? With a little creativity and ingenuity, I came up with a few tasty ways to recycle leftover* cholent.

1   BEAN SOUP

2   FREEZE IT

3   TASTES LIKE HUMUS!

4   VEGETABLE *CHOLENT* SOUP

5   BURRITOS

BEAN SOUP

Ingredients
6 Cups Water
2 Cups *Cholent*
2 Tbsp. Chicken soup mix
Cooked vegetables, noodles,
  chicken or meat (bones
  removed)
Seasoning to taste

Directions
a. Boil the water.
b. Add rest of ingredients. Cook for
    5 minutes and serve!

TASTES LIKE HUMUS!

This dish really looks like humus.

Ingredients
2 Cups *Cholent* (bones removed)
Fried onions

Directions
a. Process the *cholent* in a food
    processor or with an immersion
    blender. The mixture should be
    smooth like humus.
b. Put on a serving plate. Make an
    indentation in the middle and
    pour fried onions on top.

FREEZE IT!

Store in tightly sealed plastic
container. Label with date and
keep in freezer for future use.
Reheat with some water or soup.

VEGETABLE *CHOLENT* SOUP

Simply add some *cholent* to a
vegetable soup!

BURRITOS

This is a genius invention of mine. You must try it. People ate it by me and didn't believe it was cholent.

Ingredients

For *each* burrito:
2–3 Tbsp. *Cholent*
2 Tbsp. Tofutti cream cheese or
   parev sour cream
1 Tbsp. Ketchup

Directions

a. Put *cholent* on one side of the burrito. Spread the Tofutti and then the ketchup.

b. Roll the burrito over the mixture while folding the sides inward.

c. Fry *lightly* on both sides or warm it in the oven. (It browns quickly.)

d. Serve with lettuce and tomatoes.

⇨ *Variation*: Add a few lettuce leaves and sliced tomatoes before rolling the burrito.

LESSON 4, PART II

RICE

Here are some innovative ways to reuse cooked rice and create new and appetizing dishes.

1   RICE KUGEL

2   RICE RING

3   RICE STUFFING

4   RICE WITH MUSHROOMS

5   RICE WITH PASTRAMI

6   RICE WITH SCRAMBLED EGGS

7   RICE WITH VEGETABLES

8   SOUP WITH RICE

RICE KUGEL

Ingredients
For each cup of cooked rice:
1 Egg
1 Tbsp. Sugar
1 tsp. Vanilla
Pinch Salt
2 Tbsp. Strawberry jam

Directions
a. Mix rice with egg, sugar, vanilla, and salt.
b. Pour into a baking dish. Smooth the top.
c. Mix the jam to soften and press jam into the rice with a tablespoon. It should be visible on top.
d. Bake at 350° F for about an hour. Serve hot.

⇨ **Tip**: Fill the baking dish about ⅔ of capacity.

RICE RING

Using a ring mold provides an elegant presentation for this dish.

For a *parev* version of the Mushroom and Cheese Rice Ring from Lesson 6: Fish & Dairy, use margarine instead of butter and almond milk instead of milk. Omit the cheese.

RICE STUFFING

Use rice as a substitute (or as an added ingredient) for flour, or bread in stuffing recipes.

RICE WITH MUSHROOMS

Ingredients
2–4 Cups Cooked rice
1 Can Mushrooms (drained)
½–1 Cup Fried onions, according to taste
Seasoning, to taste
1–2 Cups Corn, peas and carrots, or other leftover vegetables

Directions
Mix all ingredients, reheat and serve.

gkrphoto/Shutterstock.com

RICE WITH PASTRAMI

The pastrami and hot dog flavor make this dish irresistible. It is a great way to get children to eat rice.

Cut some pastrami or hot dogs (or both) into small pieces and reheat with the rice.

RICE WITH SCRAMBLED EGGS

This is an unusual combination but delicious and welcome.

Ingredients
For 1 Cup rice:
1 Egg
2–3 Tbsp. Fried onions
Salt, to taste

Directions
a. Scramble eggs with a little salt.
b. Cut scrambled egg into small pieces, and set aside.
c. Reheat the rice separately.
d. Add fried onions (optional) into the rice. Mix together with the eggs.
e. Season to taste.

Delicious!

RICE WITH VEGETABLES

kariphoto/Shutterstock.com

Ingredients
Leftover rice
Leftover vegetables
Sauce

Directions
a. Put reheated rice into a mold.
b. Spread warm vegetables over rice.
c. Top with tomato or mushroom sauce (see Chicken in Sauces in Lesson 3, Section III above).

hlphoto/Shutterstock.com

SOUP WITH RICE

Add leftover rice to a soup (vegetable soup, chicken soup, tomato soup, and more).

Yulia Davidovich/Shutterstock.com

Lesson 4, Part III

PASTA

HUNGARIAN STYLE NOODLE DESSERT

A very different way of serving noodles.

Ingredients

- 1 Cup Noodles
- 3 Tbsp. Walnuts, chopped or ground
- 3 Tbsp. Sugar
- 1 tsp. Vanilla
- Optional: Add dried apricot and/or whipped cream.

Directions

a. Combine walnuts, sugar and vanilla. Mix with warm noodles.

b. Serve warm for dessert with whipped cream. Can also be served in individual ramekins.

NOODLE KUGEL

Ingredients

For each cup of noodles
1 Egg
1 Tbsp. Oil
1 Tbsp. Crushed walnuts*
1 Tbsp. Fried onions, optional
For a savory mix:
Add salt, pepper and garlic powder
   to taste
For a sweet mix:
Add 1 tablespoon sugar

* To crush walnuts, put them in
   a ziplock bag and crush with a
   rolling pin.

Directions

Mix well and bake on 350° F for 1
hour. Check center for doneness.

⇨ *Variation*: Heat a tablespoon of oil
in a pan, and fry the mixture until
one side is light brown. Turn it
over carefully and fry until light
brown. Serve immediately.

⇨ *Optional*: Garnish with sliced
apples and berries before serving.

Elena Veselova/Shutterstock.com

NOODLES REHEATED WITH EGGS

This is a simple and delicious dish. It will be an instant hit. Also, it is a great way to hide eggs for children or elderly who refused to eat eggs.

Ingredients
2 Cups Noodles
2 Eggs
Seasoning to taste

Directions
a. Beat the eggs and keep nearby.

b. Heat oil in pan. Add noodles, stirring until heated throughout.

c. Slowly pour the beaten eggs over the noodles as you continue mixing. Add seasoning. Serve hot.

NOODLES WITH BREAD CRUMBS

Noodles must be hot and drained well for this tasty recipe.

Ingredients
1 Cup Noodles
1 Tbsp. Bread crumbs
Oil, for frying
Salt, pepper, garlic powder, to taste

Directions
a. Fry bread crumbs in oil. Add seasoning. Stir until golden.

b. Add noodles. Stir until hot.

c. Toss ingredients right before serving.

⇨ *Variation*: Omit bread crumbs, and add ½ cup thawed frozen broccoli, ½ cup halved cherry tomatoes, and garnish with basil. Toss with cold noodles.

NOODLES WITH GROUND MEAT AND SAUCE

sasaken/Shutterstock.com

Ingredients

1–2 Cups Sauce
2 Cups Leftover chicken, meat, or raw ground meat*
2 Cups Noodles
Seasoning to taste

Directions

a. Prepare a sauce (See Chicken in Sauces in Lesson 3 above, for recipes) with marinara or tomato sauce.**

b. Add leftover chicken or meat pieces, or ground meat, and bring to a boil.

c. Season to taste. (If using tomato sauce, add a teaspoon of sugar and a teaspoon of lemon juice.)

d. Pour over hot noodles.

* If using raw ground meat cook until ground meat turns brown.

** Use marinara or tomato sauce without cooking up a sauce, to save time.

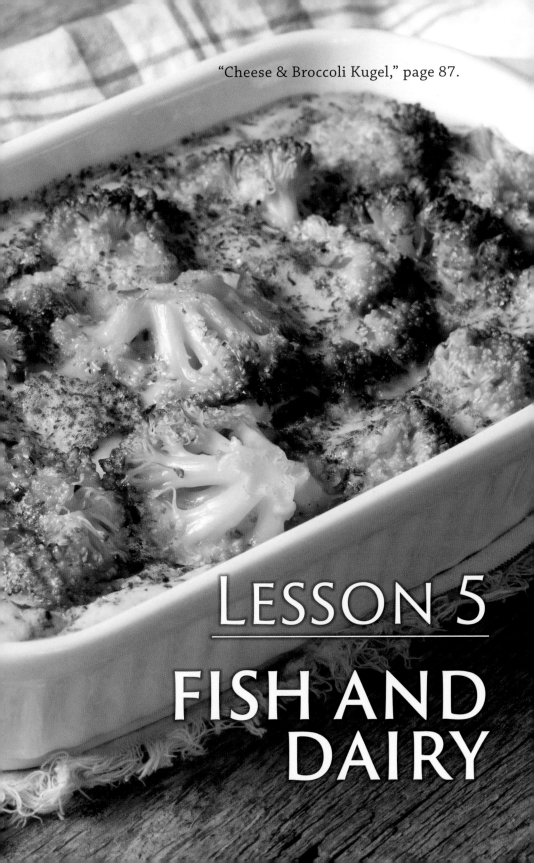

"Cheese & Broccoli Kugel," page 87.

LESSON 5

FISH AND DAIRY

Great Ways to Use Leftover Fish

Make sure to store leftover fish properly and to use it within two days, as it can spoil quickly. The fish in these recipes is without bones unless otherwise specified.

1   Fish and Potato Stew

2   Fish Balls

3   Fish Hamburgers

4   Fish in Tomato Sauce

5   Fish Soup with Wine

6   Fried Gefilte Fish

7   Reheated Fish Slices with Almond Sauce

8   Lox and Cheese Ring

9   Stuffed Peppers with Rice and Fish

FISH AND POTATO STEW

A very unusual and delicious way to use leftover fish

Ingredients

2 Cups Potatoes, cooked and cubed
3 Cups Almond or soy milk
2 Tbsp. Onions, chopped
2 Carrots, cooked and sliced
1 Can Green beans, diced and drained
1–2 Cups Cooked fish, even canned tuna
Salt, pepper, paprika and garlic powder to taste.

Directions

a. Mash 1 cup of the cooked potatoes and mix well with the milk. Set aside.
b. Put rest of ingredients, except the fish, in a large pot. Add the milk mixture and bring to a boil.
c. Taste and adjust seasoning.
d. Add the fish, simmer on low flame for 10 to 15 minutes. Serve hot.

FISH BALLS

Ingredients

1 Cup Cooked fish, crumbled
Spices
1 Egg
1 Tbsp. Matzah meal or flour

Directions

a. Crumble fish pieces very fine. You can use a potato masher.
b. Add spices, egg, and matzo meal or flour.
c. Form balls and drop them into boiling, salted water in a large pot.
d. When all of them surface in the pot, reduce heat to a low simmer. Cook for 10 minutes.
e. Remove fish balls from water and serve hot.
f. Serve with a dip or horseradish sauce.

FISH HAMBURGERS

Ingredients
1 Cup Cooked fish, crumbled
1 Whole Egg
1 Tbsp. Flour
Seasoning, to taste

Directions
a. Crumble up cooked fish or gefilte fish or combination of both and place in a bowl.

b. Add 1 egg and 1 Tbsp. flour for every cup of crumbled fish.

c. Add seasoning and mix well.

d. Shape into thin hamburgers and broil at 500°F for 10 minutes on each side or until a thin crust is formed. Serve on open hamburger bun with lettuce and tomato. Garnish with chopped parsley.

FISH IN TOMATO SAUCE

For this recipe you can leave the fish slices with the bones.

Ingredients
Sliced fish
1 Jar Marinara sauce
Olives (optional)

Directions
a. Place the slices of fish in a baking pan. Pour a jar of marinara sauce to cover the fish.

b. Adjust the seasoning.

c. Bake for about 15 minutes at 350° F or until heated through. Serve warm or cold.

Fanfo/Shutterstock.com

Bratwustle/Shutterstock.com

FISH SOUP WITH WINE

Ingredients

½ Cup Fried onions, drained
1 Lb. Frozen peas
2 Sliced cooked carrots
Salt pepper, garlic powder to taste
1 Cup Tomato sauce
1 Cup Dry white wine
2 Tbsp. *Parev* chicken soup mix
1 Cup *Parev* milk
2 Cups Cooked fish, diced

Directions

a. Put onions, peas, carrots and spices into a large pot.
b. Mix well with a hand blender.
c. Add the tomato sauce to the blended vegetables.
d. In a separate bowl, mix the *parev* chicken soup mix into the milk. Set aside.
e. Add the wine and the milk mixture into the pot. Bring to boil.
f. Add fish, simmer on low heat for 10 minutes. Serve warm.

FRIED GEFILTE FISH

Everybody likes this dish, even after Shabbat.

My friend Shterna fries slices of gefilte fish in a little oil on both sides and everybody likes it. As a variation, you can fry the gefilte fish as you would schnitzel. (See *Tips for Schnitzel* in the Chicken and Turkey Lesson.)

REHEATED FISH SLICES WITH ALMOND SAUCE

Delicious!

Ingredients
    1 Stick Butter or margarine
    6 Tbsp. Sliced almonds
    3 tsp. Mustard or mustard seeds
    2 Tbsp. Cider vinegar
    5 Tbsp. Green olives, sliced
    4 Tbsp. Water
    3–6 Slices Cooked fish, any kind

Directions
a. Sauté almonds in melted butter for a minute or two.
b. Add rest of ingredients except fish, mix and cook for 2–3 minutes.
c. Arrange fish in a flat pan, and pour the sauce over it.
d. Cover the dish and bake at 350° F for about 15 minutes or until heated through. Serve warm.

Praiwan Wasanruk/Shutterstock.com

LOX AND CHEESE RING

This recipe calls for a round ring mould dish. A loaf or round foil pan lined with plastic wrap can also be used.

Elena Shashkina/Shutterstock.com

Ingredients
    2 Lbs. Lox, sliced thin
    2 Cups Cottage cheese
    2 Cups Cream cheese
    1 Cup Hard cheese, any kind, grated
    ½ Cup Onions chopped
    ½ Cup Red pepper, diced
    ½ Cup Olives, finely chopped
    Salt, pepper, and garlic powder to taste

Directions
a. Lay the lox slices on the bottom of the ring mould dish, overlapping slices so there are no gaps. Make sure that the slices extend over the rim.

b. Mix cheese ingredients well.
c. Add onions, red pepper, olives, and seasoning to cheese mixture. Taste and adjust seasoning.
d. Press the cheese mixture into the ring on top of the salmon. Fold over the lox slices onto the cheese and carefully flip the ring onto a nice flat plate.
e. Place in the refrigerator to firm up for a half hour or overnight. Serve cold.

STUFFED PEPPERS WITH RICE AND FISH

An innovative way to use leftover cooked fish.

Ingredients

6 Peppers, any colors
2 Cups Cooked rice
½ Cup Fried onions
2 Tbsp. Oil
1 Cup Cooked fish, bones removed, cut into small pieces.
2 Tbsp. Lemon juice
Seasoning to taste
2 Cups Water mixed with
2 Tbsp. *Parev* chicken soup

Directions

a. Create cups from peppers by cutting the tops off and removing the seeds. Set aside the tops.
b. Mix rice, fried onions, oil, fish, lemon juice, and spices.
c. Stuff peppers. Place them standing up in a baking dish. Cover each stuffed pepper with the tops that were set aside in first step.
d. Combine the water and Parev chicken soup and pour around the peppers.
e. Cover and bake at 350° F about 40 minutes or until peppers are tender but still firm.
f. Serve hot.

LESSON 5, PART II

DAIRY

Tasty Ways to Use Extra Cheese.

1 CHEESE AND BROCCOLI (OR CAULIFLOWER) KUGEL

2 CHEESE AND EGGS

3 CHEESE *BOUREKAS*

4 FETA CHEESE SALAD

5 DAIRY POTATO SOUP

6 GOMBOTZ – HUNGARIAN CHEESE DUMPLINGS

7 *KOROZOTT* (HUNGARIAN CHEESE SPREAD)

8 MUSHROOMS AND CHEESE RICE RING

9 RAKOTT KRUMPLI (LAYERED POTATO CHEESE AND EGG CASSEROLE)

CHEESE AND BROCCOLI (OR CAULIFLOWER) KUGEL

Ingredients
2 lbs. Frozen Broccoli or cauliflower, defrosted
6 Eggs
2 Cups Milk
1½ Cups Grated cheese
Salt, pepper and garlic powder, to taste.

Directions
a. Drain broccoli or cauliflower, put in a bowl, set aside.
b. Mix eggs very well in a mixing bowl.
c. Cook milk stirring constantly until it reaches a boil. Remove from heat.
d. *Slowly* add eggs into the boiled milk, mixing vigorously.
e. Add cheese and spices.
f. Pour the milk mixture into a 9" × 13" pan, and then add the broccoli or cauliflower. Bake at 350° F for an hour or until a toothpick inserted in center comes out dry. Serve hot.

CHEESE AND EGGS

There are many ways to use up cheese with eggs. (See the Frittata and Kugel recipes in Lesson 3 above and Lesson 6 below.)

Here are some quick and easy suggestions:

⇨ Scramble eggs with some leftover grated hard cheese, add seasoning and chopped parsley with a slice of toast for a delicious meal that incorporates three food groups.

⇨ Scramble eggs. Put grated cheese on one side of the egg and flip the egg over the cheese.

⇨ Add cooked vegetables into the grated cheese and proceed with an omelet or scrambled egg.

⇨ Fry the egg very thinly. Remove from heat. Spread cream cheese on one side and roll up the egg.

⇨ Prepare any of the eggs above. Return to the frying pan and pour tomato sauce or marinara sauce over the egg. Reheat for 5 minutes.

CHEESE BOUREKAS

Ingredients

- 1 Package Frozen mini bourekas
- 1 Egg
- 1 Cup Cheese, any kind, can be a mix
- Seasoning, to taste

Directions

a. Defrost mini frozen *bourekas*.
b. Mix the cheeses, egg and seasoning.
c. Fill the bourekas with cheese mixture, about 1 teaspoon per *boureka*.
d. Bake for 15–20 minutes at 350° F. Serve warm.
   Yields about 10 to 12 bourekas.

FETA CHEESE SALAD

Ingredients

- 1 lb. Feta cheese, crumbled
- 2 Red peppers, rinsed and cubed
- 1 tsp. Black pepper
- For the dressing:
- 4 Tbsp. Oil
- 4 Tbsp. Apple cider vinegar
- 8 Tbsp. Water
- Salt, garlic powder
- Mix well until mixture turns cloudy.

Directions

a. Arrange feta cheese in a nice dish. Sprinkle with black pepper.
b. Cut red pepper into small pieces and spread over the feta.
c. Prepare dressing by mixing until the dressing turns cloudy. Pour over feta and serve immediately.

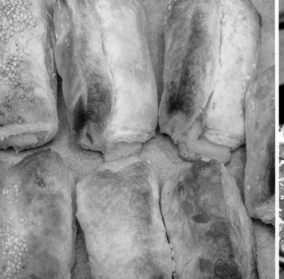

DAIRY POTATO SOUP

I still remember my mother cooking this soup and adding the sour cream right before serving.

Ingredients

6 Potatoes, peeled and cubed
2–3 Cups Milk
3 Tbsp. *Parev* chicken soup powder
2 Onions, chopped and lightly fried
4 Tbsp. Flour
1 tsp. Paprika
4 Tbsp. Water
1 Tbsp. Oil
½–1 Cup Sour cream
Salt and pepper, to taste

Directions

a. Boil the potatoes in a pot of water until tender but firm, and drain.

b. Put milk in a pot, add the parev chicken soup powder, and mix well.

c. Add the potatoes and lightly fried onions to the milk. Bring to a boil and season.

d. Mix flour, paprika, water and oil in a separate bowl, until smooth. Add a ladleful of the hot milk into the flour mixture and pour back into the pot of potatoes and onions. Cook another 15 minutes to half an hour. Remove from heat.

e. Right before serving, add the sour cream to the soup and mix well.

nada54/Shutterstock.com

GOMBOTZ – HUNGARIAN CHEESE DUMPLINGS

Ingredients

- 2 lbs Farmer cheese
- 5 Eggs
- ¾ Cup Farina
- 2 Tbsp. Butter, melted
- 4 Tbsp. Flour
- 1 tsp. Salt
- ½ Cup Sugar
- 5 Tbsp. Bread crumbs mixed with 2 Tbsp. oil

Directions

a. Combine the cheese, eggs, farina and melted butter, flour, and salt. Mix well.

b. Chill in the refrigerator for half an hour.

c. Put up a large pot of water to boil. Salt lightly. Form balls from the cheese mixture, making sure they are tightly formed. When the water boils, drop them in, one by one.

d. After the balls surface, cook for another 5 minutes. Turn off the fire and remove the dumplings very carefully using a strainer.

e. Prepare bread crumbs with 2 Tablespoons of oil, and ½ cup of sugar in a frying pan. Stir for a minute and transfer to a flat plate.

f. Take dumplings one by one and roll around in bread crumbs. Serve immediately.

marinart1/Shutterstock.com

KOROZOTT (HUNGARIAN CHEESE SPREAD)

Don't try to pronounce the name because it is very Hungarian but it is a great spread and well worth adding to your repertoire.

Ingredients
1 Cup Cream cheese
1 Cup Farmer cheese
½ Cup Cottage cheese (optional)
2 Tbsp. Paprika
1 Cup Onion, finely chopped
Salt to taste
Caraway seeds (optional)

Directions
a. Mix all ingredients, form a log and serve.
b. Can be eaten as is or spread on toast or bread.

MUSHROOM AND CHEESE RICE RING

This delicious recipe is also a feast for the eyes. It requires a round deep ring dish (which can be disposable).

Ingredients
1 Cup Onions, fried in butter or oil, and drained
3 Cups Cooked rice
3 Eggs, beaten
1½ Cups Milk
3 Tbsp. Parsley, chopped
Salt, pepper, and garlic powder, to taste
2 Cups Hard cheese, grated
1 Can Mushrooms, sliced and drained
1 Can Peas and carrots, drained
1 tsp. Mustard
1 Red pepper, cut into small pieces and cooked in a little water for 2 minutes, drained.
5 Tbsp. Bread crumbs mixed with 2 Tbsp. oil
1 tsp. Paprika

For the roux
4 Tbsp. Flour
4 Tbsp. Oil
2 cups Water

Directions
a. Put half of the fried onions in a mixing bowl and add the cooked rice.
b. Mix eggs and milk together and

add to the rice mixture.

c. Add parsley, seasoning and 1½ cups of the grated cheese.

d. Generously grease a ring mold, pour in the rice mixture, and press it down. Bake for an hour at 350° F.

e. Remove from oven and turn onto a large serving dish.

f. Prepare 1 cup of a basic roux sauce (see Chicken in Sauces in Lesson 3).

g. Add the mushrooms, peas and carrots, drained and cooked red pepper, mustard and seasoning and other half of fried onions to the roux. Cook for about 5 minutes until all vegetables are heated through.

h. Pour the vegetable roux mixture into center of ring. Top with bread crumbs mixture and remaining ½ cup of grated cheese. Sprinkle with paprika. Serve hot.

See Rice Ring recipe above in Lesson 4: Cholent, Rice and Pasta, for a parev version.

Yehuda Boltshauser/Kuvien Images

RAKOTT KRUMPLI

This is another Hungarian staple and true comfort food. My mother used to prepare this in a ring form but it comes out delicious in a casserole dish too. Using butter pieces in between the layers will guarantee this to be scrumptious. My mother used to say, "if it is not delicious don't eat it." Enjoy indulging in this delicious dish for a special occasion.

Ingredients
6 Potatoes, cooked in salted water and drained
6 Eggs, hardboiled
2 sticks Butter (maybe more)
½ lb. Hard cheese, sliced
Salt, pepper, and garlic powder

For the sauce:
5 Tbsp. Oil
2–3 Tbsp. Flour
1 Cup Water
1 tsp. Paprika, and seasoning to taste

Directions
a. Slice potatoes and set aside. Slice eggs and set aside. Separate slices of hard cheese.

b. Generously grease a casserole dish. Layer potato slices and dot with butter. Sprinkle lightly with spices. Lay sliced eggs on top of potatoes and then the cheese. Repeat layers and spices, dotting with butter in between layers. Finish with a layer of potato and butter.

c. Prepare the sauce (See Chicken in Sauces in Lesson 3 for directions) and pour on top. Sprinkle with paprika. Bake for 35–40 minutes at 350° F until golden. Serve hot.

⇨ *Variation:* Spread fried onions on every potato layer. Finish with potato and butter on top.

LESSON 6
FRUITS AND VEGETABLES

LESSON 6, PART I

FRUIT

The following recipes can be used for leftover fruits and vegetables. Some of the recipes use raw vegetables and some use cooked ingredients.

1 APPLE SAUCE

2 FRUIT FRITTERS

3 FRUIT PIE

4 FRUIT SALAD WITH BALSAMIC VINEGAR TOPPING

5 FRUIT SMOOTHIE

6 FRUITS IN SYRUP

7 ICE-POPS

8 LEMON PUDDING WITH PEARS OR APPLES

9 ORANGE SECTIONS AND BANANA CASSEROLE

APPLE SAUCE

Once you try this recipe you will always want to have apples on hand in order to make it over and over.

Ingredients
5 Apples, cored, peeled and cut into eighths

Directions
a. Spread apple pieces in a 9" × 13" pan and bake, uncovered, for about 1 ½ hours at 400° F or until apples are very soft.
b. Remove from oven, let cool and puree the apples in the food processor.
Yields about 6 portions

Note: Since the apples are baked uncovered some of the pieces might have burnt edges. Remove those black edges before putting the apples into the food processor.

I do not add any sugar and everybody likes it. You can add sugar to taste if you like.

⇨ *Variation*: My daughter Michal prepares the apples as above, and puts them in a 9" × 13" pan. She adds some other fruits like prunes, pineapple, peaches. (If you use canned fruits, drain them). Bake covered for about 1 ½ hours. Mash the large pieces. Serve warm or cold.

FRUIT FRITTERS

This is a delicious snack my mother used to prepare with apples. However, you can use any hard fruit.

Ingredients:

2 Cups Apples, pears, pineapples, melons or other hard fruit, peeled, cored, and cut into ½" slices
2 Cups Flour
2–3 Eggs, beaten
½ tsp. Salt
2 Tbsp. Oil (plus oil for frying)
4 Tbsp. Sugar
½ tsp. Cinnamon (optional)

Directions

a. Mix all ingredients except fruit, in a bowl. The batter has to have a consistency of buttermilk, so that when you dip the fruits, it shouldn't slide off the fruits. If it is too thick, add a few drops of water, and if it is too "runny," add a tablespoon of flour.
b. Heat oil in a frying pan.
c. Dip each slice of fruit in batter and drop gently into the hot oil to fry. Turn the slices when edges become light brown, and fry the other side for about a minute. Remove fruit with a slotted spoon and transfer to a plate lined with paper towels.

Optional: Sprinkle fritters with confectioner's sugar. Serve warm.

FRUIT PIE

Ingredients

9" Ready pie crust*
1 Cup Fruit such as banana, pears, apples, cherries or a mixture
½ Cup Sugar
½ Cup Flour
2 Cups *Parev* milk like soy or almond, or regular milk
4 Egg yolks
Whipped cream, optional

Directions

a. In a medium pot, combine sugar, flour, and milk and bring to a boil.
b. In a separate small bowl mix the egg yolks thoroughly, add a little of the hot flour mixture into the egg yolks mixture while mixing vigorously, adding the rest of the flour mixture to the eggs, a little at a time. Then transfer the egg

yolk and flour mixture to the pot.

c. Add a little at a time, mixing thoroughly with a whisk, and cook for about 1 minute, over low fire.
d. Add the cup of fruits and cook for a minute or 2. Let cool a bit and pour into the pie shell.
e. Bake for 30 minutes at 350° F.
f. Leave in oven until center is firm.
g. Can be topped with whipped cream when completely cooled.

* *If using frozen unbaked pie crust, pierce pie crust with a fork. Cover pie crust with some raw beans to keep the crust flat while baking. Bake pie shell in the oven at 350° F for 20 minutes.*

FRUIT SALAD

a. Simply cut up any fruits available into bite sized pieces.
b. For every cup of fruit, add ¼ cup orange juice or a drizzle of liquor for a kick.
c. You can add some cinnamon or for a completely different taste sprinkle fruit with 1–2 Tablespoons of balsamic vinegar to every cup of fruit.

FRUIT SMOOTHIE

Directions

a. In blender, combine ⅓ cup orange juice, water or milk for every cup of fruit.
b. Blend until smooth.
c. Pour into glasses and enjoy.
   Yields 1 serving

Optional: Add some sugar or liquor to taste.

Vitalina Rybakova/Shutterstock.com

FRUITS IN SYRUP

Ingredients

½ Cup Sugar
½ Cup Water
1" Slice Fresh ginger (optional)
1 Tbsp. Lime or lemon rind

Directions

a. Cook all ingredients together until mixture thickens a bit.

gkrphoto/Shutterstock.com

b. Add a piece of ginger (optional).
c. Add Lime or lemon rind into the syrup.
d. Pour syrup over cut up fruits and serve.

⇨ *Variation*: Add 2–3 Tbsp. crushed or ground almonds or walnuts.

Squeeze 1 Tbsp. lemon juice on top of fruits.

Grandview Graphics/Shutterstock.com

ICE-POPS

a. Use the smoothie recipe to make ice-pops too.
b. Pour into plastic cups with a stick inserted to use as a popsicle stick, or pour into ices containers and freeze until firm.

Elena Shashkina/Shutterstock.com

LEMON PUDDING WITH PEARS OR APPLES

Ingredients
2 Pears or apples
½ Cup Cookie crumbs
⅓ Cup Chopped nuts
¼ Cup Brown sugar
2 Tbsp. Margarine or oil
1 Package Instant lemon pudding

Directions
a. Grate pears or apples.
b. Mix cookie crumbs, nuts, sugar, and margarine well.
c. Mix in the fruit.
d. Prepare the pudding as directed on package.
e. Alternate layers of nut mixture and pudding in a glass bowl. Refrigerate before serving.

JLwarehouse/Shutterstock.com

ORANGE SECTIONS AND BANANA CASSEROLE

oxyzay/Shutterstock.com

Ingredients

8 Over-ripe bananas, mashed
1 Small Can Orange sections
½ Cup Sugar
4 Tbsp. Liquid from the can of fruit
1 Cup Cookie crumbs

Directions

a. Mix all ingredients besides cookie crumbs.
b. Pour into a greased baking dish. Cover with crumbs and bake for 40 minutes at 350° F.

LESSON 6, PART II

VEGETABLES

CREATIVE WAYS TO USE COOKED VEGETABLES

Many times we have small amounts of cooked vegetables left over. If there isn't enough to serve a whole family, here are some creative ways to use these tasty and healthy leftovers.

☑ Mix them into hamburgers before cooking.

☑ Add them to a *cholent* or bean stew.

☑ Prepare *bourekas* and mix some leftover vegetables with mashed potato. (Each *boureka* needs about 1 Tablespoon of filling.)

☑ Mix in some leftover eggplant or letcho or any other small amount of cooked vegetables into a wrap. Serve fried or heated in the oven.

☑ Add some cooked vegetables to a pot of fresh vegetable soup.

☑ Add it to a wrap that you are going to serve with other ingredients, such as ground meat or grated cheese.

☑ Add it to the stuffing for chicken or turkey.

☑ Add it to a roast that you are cooking in the oven.

DAIRY POTATO SOUP
(See Lesson 5: Fish and Dairy for recipe)

FISH AND POTATO SOUP
(See Lesson 5: Fish and Dairy for recipe)

GAZPACHO

Gazpacho is a cold soup and very refreshing on a hot summer night. Best of all, it is a great solution for a day old Israeli salad.

Directions

a. Pour ½ cup tomato sauce generously over 1 cup Israeli salad.
b. Use an immersion blender to mix all ingredients.
c. Add salt, pepper and garlic powder to taste and a teaspoon of sugar.
d. Chill for a few hours and serve very cold.

LETCHO (HUNGARIAN THICK VEGETABLE STEW)

I mentioned Letcho several times in this book.

The basic recipe calls for diced peppers, fried onions, and tomatoes.

But you can add some grated carrots, grated parsnip, broccoli, cauliflower, or even green beans. As long as you can use up some leftovers vegetables and save them from being thrown away!

MASHED POTATOES

You must try this simple and delicious recipe.

Ingredients

    5 Potatoes, cooked
    ½ Cup Clear Soup, or hot water
    ½ Cup Oil
    Salt, pepper and garlic powder, to
        taste

Directions

a. Transfer strained potatoes just removed from the cooking pot into a bowl.
b. Add rest of ingredients and mash with potato masher.
c. Taste, adjust seasoning, and serve hot.

⇨ **Tip:** Always use hot potatoes straight from cooking for mashed potatoes. Once they cooled off you won't achieve the desired smooth consistency. Hot water from the liquid of the cooked potato, or clear chicken soup, can be added to desired consistency.

PICKLED VEGETABLES

Ingredients

    4 Cups Assorted cooked vegetables,
        sliced
    1 Cup Vinegar
    2 Cups Water
    2 Cups Sugar
    2 Tbsp. Salt, or more to taste
    Bay leaf and pickling spices,
        optional

Directions

a. Bring all ingredients, except for the cooked vegetables, to a boil.
b. Pour over cooked and sliced vegetables such as onions, carrots, cauliflower, parsnip, sliced cabbage, cucumbers, whole garlic cloves, peppers (any color), or beets. (Warning: beets will dye all other vegetables in the mix, red). Let cool.
c. For best results, strain the liquid you just poured on the vegetables, re-boil the strained liquid and pour over the vegetables again.
d. These vegetables can be mixed together or separated by kind. When cool, store in glass jars. Can be kept refrigerated for up to a month.

Melica/Shutterstock.com

MaraZe/Shutterstock.com

POTATO HASH BROWNS

Ingredients
   4 Potatoes, cooked and cubed
   ½ Cup Onions, fried
   1 Tbsp. Oil
   Salt and pepper to taste

Directions
a. Combine potatoes and onions.
b. Heat oil in pan and fry potatoes and onions until most of the potatoes are light brown, turning occasionally. Serve hot.

POTATOES WITH FRIED ONIONS

When short on time, this alternative to the Potato Hash Browns recipe above can be made quickly.

Ingredients
   4 Potatoes, cooked and cubed
   ½ Cup Onions, fried
   Salt and pepper to taste

Directions
a. Combine potatoes and onions. Season to taste.

POTATO KUGEL

Using leftover mashed potatoes
This recipe can be doubled and tripled.

Ingredients
　　1 Cup Mashed potatoes (see
　　　　Mashed Potato recipe above)
　　1 Egg
　　1 Tbsp. Oil
　　Salt, pepper and garlic, to taste

Directions
　a.　Mix all ingredients well.
　b.　Fill a well-oiled baking dish up to
　　　an inch from the top.
　c.　Sprinkle with bread crumbs on top.
　d.　Drizzle some oil on top.
　e.　Bake at 350° F for one hour.

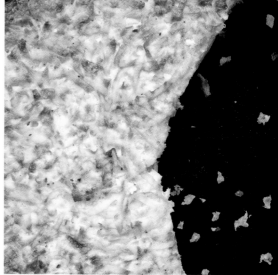

Margoe Edwards/Shutterstock.com

POTATO SALAD

Foodio/Shutterstock.com

Ingredients
　　4 potatoes, cooked and cubed
　　4 carrots, cooked and diced
　　2 Pickles, diced
　　3–5 Tbsp. Mayonnaise
　　½ Onion, chopped (optional)
　　Salt, pepper, and garlic powder, to
　　　taste

Directions
　　Mix all ingredients and serve at
　　room temperature.

ROASTED VEGETABLES

Ingredients

Raw root vegetables, enough to cover a large cookie sheet. Can be any combination of carrots, parsnip, kohlrabi, onions, eggplant, zucchini, and peppers. (If using peppers, cut them into strips before broiling, and peel them after broiling.)

Oil spray

Marinade

2 Cups Water

1 Cup Vinegar

½ Cup Oil

2 Tbsp. Salt

2 Tbsp. Garlic, freshly grated

Directions

a. Spread sliced, raw root vegetables on a greased cookie sheet in a single layer.

b. Spray some oil on them and broil for about 15 minutes.*

c. Put the vegetables in a large jar or jars. Do not overstuff.

d. Prepare the marinade in another jar, mixing vigorously.

e. Pour marinade over vegetables. Refrigerate for a few hours or overnight.

* I recommend broiling each type of vegetable separately, as each one may require different cooking time.

➪ *Variation*: My cousin Dassi suggests a shorter way: Cut peppers into thin long strips about ½" each. Spread the cut peppers in a baking dish. Bake at 400° F for 15 minutes. Remove from oven and let cool. Put in a jar and pour marinade over the peppers. This saves you the peeling of the peppers.

Robyn Mackenzie/Shutterstock.com

ROAST WITH VEGETABLES

You can add any cooked vegetables to a roast.

Directions

a. Arrange the cooked vegetables around the roast.

b. Use the same spices on the roast and on the vegetables.

c. Once the roast is cooked, pour the liquid off while the roast is still hot. This way the vegetables will not swim in fat.

d. Pour the liquid into a glass jar and refrigerate.

e. Once the liquid jells, remove the fat and use the flavorful disk that formed in the bottom of the jar to reheat the roast in. If you don't need it for the roast, you can use this jelled liquid to start a soup, to flavor pasta, or to add flavor to a *cholent*.

SAUERKRAUT

Here is a recipe if you have a lot of cabbage in the house. The taste is much milder than bought sauerkraut and it is very easy to do. Try it.

Directions

a. Shred the cabbage and put it into a jar.

b. Add 1 tablespoon of salt for every cup of shredded cabbage. Mix well. Try to put something heavy on top of the cabbage to press it down, like a heavy can.

c. Cover tightly and let stand on the counter for 3 days. Then refrigerate.

d. Use it as an accompaniment for meat or chicken, considered to be very healthy.

VEGETABLE CASEROLE

Ingredients
2 Tbsp. Oil
½ Cup Bread crumbs
4 Cups Cooked carrots, sliced any way you prefer
1½ Cups Sauce (see Chicken in Sauces in Lesson 3, Section III, for directions)
1 Cup Crumbled tofu

Directions
a. Heat oil in a frying pan.
b. Add bread crumbs and toss to absorb all of the oil. Keep tossing so bread crumbs do not burn. Remove from fire once they are a golden color. Set aside on a plate.
c. In a separate bowl, combine the carrots, sauce and tofu.
d. Pour the mixture into a greased baking dish, smooth the mixture down, sprinkle bread crumbs mixture over it.
e. Bake for 30 minutes on 350° F. Serve hot.

⇨ *Variation*: Instead of carrots, use cooked strained broccoli, cauliflower, green beans, sliced celery or any other cooked vegetables.

⇨ *Variation*: Cubed boneless chicken, meat, or cubed salami can be added to the vegetable mixture.

VEGETABLE FRITTATA

For every 10 eggs use 1½ cups of any assortment of cooked vegetables like carrots, parsnip, eggplant, cabbage, cauliflower, broccoli, etc.

Directions
a. Mix eggs with salt pepper garlic powder.
b. Pour into a large oiled frying pan let cook 2 minutes
c. Add the cooked, chopped, vegetables.
d. Lower the heat and cook until the middle of the frittata sets. Do not overcook.
Optional: Some shredded cheese can be sprinkled on top before serving.

Chudovska/Shutterstock.com
Igor Dutina/Shutterstock.com

VEGETABLE FRITTERS

a. Use the recipe for fruit fritters (above), omitting the sugar, and adding 2 teaspoons of salt.

b. Cut ½ inch slices of raw vegetables, such as carrots, zucchini, mushrooms cauliflower, broccoli, parsnip, asparagus or celery (peeled and cut into 1 inch pieces), eggplant, kohlrabi, or even slices of onions. Make sure you pat them dry.

c. Dip in batter and fry on both sides. Serve hot.

Optional: Add shredded cheese and/or dip into bread crumbs.

VEGETABLE KUGEL

Ingredients
4 Cups Assorted cooked vegetables
4 Eggs
2 Tbsp. Oil
½ Cup *Parev* milk
4 Tbsp. Flour
Salt, pepper, and garlic powder to taste

Directions
a. Mash the cooked vegetables, add beaten eggs, oil, *parev* milk, and flour.
b. Mix well and pour into a 9" × 13" pan. Bake at 350° F for about an hour or until top appears golden and is not liquidy.

Note: This recipe can be prepared with only one vegetable, like carrots, or with a mixture of vegetables. If using cooked celery, slice before adding to the other vegetables.

VEGETABLE PIE

Ingredients
9 inch Unbaked pie crust
2 Cups Mashed cooked vegetables,
  such as potato, sweet potato,
  carrots, etc.
4 Eggs, beaten
3 Tbsp. Oil
2 Tbsp. Flour
1 Cup *Parev* milk
Salt, pepper, and garlic powder to
  taste

Directions
a. Pierce pie crust with a fork in a
    few places. Bake at 375° F for 15
    minutes and let cool.
b. Mix all ingredients. Pour mixture
    into pie shell and bake for 45
    minutes at 350° F.

Optional: Add some bread crumbs on
    top or grated hard cheese, for a
    dairy vegetable pie.

VEGETABLE SOUP

*A very good way to use a lot of vegetables
is in a soup. Any vegetable can go into
this soup. Even tomatoes and lettuce
from last night's salad!*

a. Bring a large pot filled with
    water to a boil. Meanwhile cut all
    vegetables to bite size pieces.
b. Add the vegetables and simmer
    on low.
c. Cook for about an hour.
d. Mix in 2 Tablespoons flour mixed
    with ¼ cup of cold water. Add
    spices. Serve hot.

⇨ *Variation*: Mash all vegetables
    with an immersion blender. Make
    sure that the flame is shut off
    when you use the hand mixer.

LESSON 7

CHALLAH, BREAD, AND CAKE

"Baked Garlic Challah," page 117.

LESSON 7, PART I

BEING CREATIVE WITH *CHALLAH* & BREAD

Here is an amazing list of dishes that you can create with either leftover challah *or bread.*

1   BAKED GARLIC *CHALLAH*

2   BREAD CRUMBS

3   *CHALLAH* CUBES BAKED IN CUSTARD

4   CHOCOLATE "CAKE"

5   CHOPPED LIVER

6   CROUTONS

7   FRENCH TOAST

8   FRIED SEASONED *CHALLAH*

9   HAMBURGER AND MEATBALL HELPERS

10 SANDWICHES

11 STUFFING

12 TOASTED GARLIC *CHALLAH*

13 VEGETABLE KUGEL

BAKED GARLIC *CHALLAH*

Brent Hofacker/Shutterstock.com

Ingredients
1 *Challah*, whole
1 Tbsp. each Garlic powder, chopped parsley, oregano, dried dill
½ Tbsp. Salt
¾ Cup Margarine or butter, melted
Optional: Grated cheese

Directions
a. Slice *challah* about ¾ of the way down each slice, not cutting all the way through, leaving the bottom uncut.
b. Mix all ingredients and drizzle in between the slices. Make sure both sides of slices are covered with the spicy mixture.
c. Place the challah into a rectangle baking pan. Bake at 300° F for about 20 minutes.

BREAD CRUMBS

Directions
a. Put leftover challah in a paper bag and store in a dry place. Let it dry.
b. Process the challah into bread crumbs with a food processor.

If the challah is still soft, use in recipes calling for "panko."
c. Use the bread crumbs in dishes that call for bread crumbs and count the money you saved.

CHALLAH CUBES BAKED IN CUSTARD

This and the "Chocolate Cake" below are so delicious that you will be tempted to bake extra challah just to have enough to make them for dessert.

Ingredients

1 Stick Margarine, melted (8 ounces)
1 Cup Sugar
3 Cups Almond or soy milk (*parev*)
4 Eggs
½ tsp. Salt
1 tsp. Vanilla
4 Cups *Challah*, cut in cubes

Directions

a. Cook the margarine with sugar and almond milk until blended well. Set aside to cool.
b. In a large bowl, beat eggs by hand. Stir in salt and vanilla.
c. Slowly add milk mixture to eggs, while mixing vigorously.
d. Spread *challah* cubes in a greased 9" × 13" pan. Pour milk mixture over them. Some of the challah will float to the top.
e. Bake for about an hour on 350° F. Take out of oven when an inserted toothpick comes out dry.

CHOCOLATE "CAKE"

I wrote "cake" in quotation marks because the whole recipe is made from challah but you can fool anyone with this "secret" ingredient.

Ingredients:
For a 9" × 13" pan:

7 Cups Challah, left to dry in paper bag at least a week, cut into small cubes.

2½ Cups Sugar

½ Cup Oil

1 Cup Milk (*parev*)

8 eggs Beaten

10 oz. Chocolate, cut in small pieces and melted

1 tsp. Vanilla

Directions

a. Place dry challah cubes in a shallow pan. Pour milk over it. Let challah absorb the milk.

b. Melt the chocolate. (If you use the microwave, make sure not to burn the chocolate.)

c. Gently pour the melted chocolate over the challah mixture.

d. Combine the eggs, sugar, oil and vanilla in a separate bowl. Stir into the challah/chocolate mixture gently to retain the shape of the challah cubes.

e. Pour into a greased 9"x13" pan and bake for an hour at 350° F.

f. Check for doneness. If a toothpick removed from center is wet, continue baking for another 10 minutes.

Enjoy! The *bracha* on this cake is *mezonot*.

CHOPPED LIVER

My mother made the best chopped liver. Her secret was the day old challah she used, and the meat grinder. Today you can get a grinder as an attachment for your main mixer. Just please don't use a food processor for this recipe!

Ingredients:
1 ½ lb. Kosher chicken livers
2 Eggs, boiled
1 medium Onion, fried in oil.
  (Don't drain the oil.)
2–3 slices Challah, soaked in water
  then squeezed
To taste: Salt, pepper, and garlic
  powder

Directions
a. Grind the ingredients one after the other. Make sure to use some of the oil with the fried onions.

b. Mix and put through the grinder 2 more times.

c. Adjust spices, mix and call me to tell me how it came out.

TalyaAL/Shutterstock.com

CROUTONS

Danny Smythe/Shutterstock.com

Ingredients
10 Slices *Challah* or bread, cut into
  small cubes
1 Tbsp. Each salt, garlic powder,
  black pepper

Directions
a. Spray cubed *challah* or bread with Pam.

b. In a separate bowl mix 1 tablespoon of each: salt, garlic powder and black pepper. Sprinkle over the croutons, and mix well.

c. Spread out on a lined baking sheet and bake in the oven at 350° F.

d. Check after 5 minutes. If not golden, continue to bake for another 5 minutes.

e. Cool and serve as is or sprinkled over salads.

⇨ *Variation*: Use oregano and basil for Italian croutons. For a *milchig* version, sprinkle with grated cheese before baking.

FRENCH TOAST

Ingredients

4 Slices *Challah*, ½" thick
1 Cup Milk, or parev milk, divided
    into two ½ Cups
4 Eggs, beaten
Oil for frying (Enough to coat
    bottom of pan.)

Directions

a. Dip the *challah* slices in a bowl
   with ½ cup milk.
b. Beat eggs with the other ½ cup
   milk and dip the slices into the
   egg mixture.
c. Fry in hot oil.
d. Turn when it is light brown
   around the edges. Fry on the
   other side and remove to a plate
   with paper towels.
e. Can be eaten as is or with some
   coarse salt sprinkled on top. Serve
   hot.

⇨ *Variation*: Sprinkle generously
with powdered sugar and
cinnamon.

FRIED SEASONED *CHALLAH*

Ingredients

4 slices *Challah*
2 Tbsp. Butter or margarine,
   melted
Fresh parsley, oregano, garlic, salt
   to taste

Directions

a. Brush slices of bread or *challah*
   with melted butter or margarine.

b. Fry on both sides.

c. Sprinkle with fresh parsley or
   oregano, garlic powder and salt.

Africa Studio/Shutterstock.com

argouillat photo/Shutterstock.com

HAMBURGER AND MEATBALL HELPERS

I always add a little soaked and squeezed challah to my hamburger or meat ball mixture with or without bread crumbs. Just make sure to cut the squeezed challah into small pieces before you mix it in.

Moving Moment/Shutterstock.com

SANDWICHES

Use leftover *challah* and day old bread for the sandwiches you prepare for lunch.

Put a generous amount of mayonnaise or cream cheese (for a dairy

sandwich) and proceed with your sandwich. It can be filled with leftover vegetables or, for a meat sandwich, leftover chicken. Don't be apologetic about using day old bread. It is delicious as a sandwich.

STUFFING

When you prepare stuffing for a turkey or a chicken you can always add some soaked and squeezed challah. Adjust seasoning. Good for any recipe of stuffing. I personally use up the vegetables from the soup as well as the left over challah or bread.

Ingredients
    1 Cup Root vegetables, cooked
    1 Slice Bread or *challah*
    1 Whole Egg
    Salt, pepper and garlic powder

Directions
a. For a turkey I would use about 3–4 cups of stuffing and for a chicken, 2 cups.
b. Season generously with salt, pepper and garlic powder.
c. If all the stuffing does not fit into the bird bake it around it in the pan.

TOASTED GARLIC *CHALLAH*

This recipe brings me back to my childhood memories of my mother toasting challah on Motzei Shabbat.

Ingredients
Challah
Fresh garlic
Butter

Directions
Spread fresh garlic and butter on toasted leftover sliced *challah*. Simple and delicious.

nargouillat photo/Shutterstock.com

VEGETABLE KUGEL

Challah is a fine substitute for flour in a vegetable kugel. Simply soak the *challah* slices in water, squeeze excess liquid and cut into small pieces.

Use one slice of *challah* for every cup of assorted vegetables, one egg, and seasoning to taste.

3–4 cups will be enough for a 9" × 13" pan. For smaller baking pans make sure to fill ⅔ of the pan. Always spray the pan in advance.

Marie C Fields/Shutterstock.com

LESSON 7, PART II

CREATING TASTY DESSERTS WITH LEFTOVER CAKE

So many times we are stock with leftover cake and cookies. When we are having a party or friends and family over, we have these leftovers. The best thing to do is to store the cake away in the freezer for later use.

Once you planning to bake a cake, first check what do you have in the freezer and create new dishes from the leftovers. All amounts and ingredients given here can be changed, added or reduced according to taste.

1   "BAKED ALASKA" WITH CAKE BASE

2   BAKED PIE SHELL

3   CAKE CRUMBS

4   CAKE LOLLIPOPS

5   EGGNOG CAKE

6   ICE-CREAM CAKE

7   LAYER CAKE

8   RUM BALLS

9   SHAPE-A-CAKE

10   TRIFLE

"BAKED ALASKA" WITH CAKE BASE

BAKED PIE SHELL

Use a layer of a round left over cake. Pour a can of cherry pie filling over it. Cover the cake with a ring of whipped cream which was mixed with ½ cup sugar. The cherry pie filling should be exposed in the middle. To be very fancy you can create some peeks in the whipped cream and burn the edges with a little kitchen torch. Be careful not to melt the whipped cream.

You may use cake crumbs as a pie shell especially when a recipe calls for graham crackers crumbs.

Mix about 2 cups of cake crumbs with ½ stick of softened margarine and ½ cup of sugar. Press mixture into the pie pan. Proceed to fill the pie shell. Baked or unbaked.

thefoodphotographer/Shutterstock.com

Lesya Dolyuk/Shutterstock.com

CAKE CRUMBS

Crumble cake into small crumbs. (You can use a food processor for this step.) Put on a cookie sheet and bake for 10 minutes. Let cool, store in a closed container, and sprinkle over ice cream or fruit salad before serving.

CAKE LOLLIPOPS

Agnes Kantaruk/Shutterstock.com

Use the mixture for rum balls below. Make sure the mixture is firm. Form balls and poke a lollipop stick into each one. Decorate (optional) or dip in melted chocolate and serve on a fancy doily.

➪ *Variation*: Cover the lollipops with melted chocolate and sprinkles.

Ildi Papp/Shutterstock.com

EGGNOG CAKE

The eggnog sauce is delicious. Once you master this technique you will want to use it in many recipes.

Ingredients

Leftover cake cut into 10–20 individual squares. (Pour the sauce on the ones you serve immediately)

4 Cups White wine
6   Egg yolks
2 Cups Sugar
1 tsp. Vanilla

Directions

a. Mix the egg yolks in a bowl. Set aside.

b. Combine the wine and sugar in a large pot and bring to a boil. Cook for about 5 minutes.

c. Slowly pour a *few drops* at a time of the hot mixture into the egg yolks, while mixing the egg yolks vigorously. Continuing until most of the wine mixture is incorporated.

d. Pour the mixture back in the pot and cook on low flame, mixing constantly. (This is not the time to answer the phone!)

e. Remove from heat when the sauce is thick and shiny.

f. Pour on cake and serve. Can be used hot or cold.

ICE CREAM CAKE

YaiSirichai/Shutterstock.com

Directions

a. Line a round pan with parchment paper.
b. Press some cake slices on bottom.
c. Drizzle with 2 Tablespoons of wine.
d. Cover evenly with your favorite ice cream.
e. Repeat (*optional*). Freeze.
f. Turn cake onto a serving plate.
g. Sprinkle with chocolate sprinkles or drizzle with melted chocolate.
h. Return to freezer to firm up. Serve cold.

LAYER CAKE

By adding a base layer of leftover cake crumbs you can create this delicious dessert.

Ingredients

5–6 Cups Leftover cake and cookies, processed in a food processor.

For Glaze:

6 heaping Tbsp. Cocoa
1 Cup Water
¾ Cup Sugar
1 Stick Margarine, room temperature
2 tsp. Vanilla
6 Tbsp. Liquor (any kind)
9" Round Sponge cake

Yehuda Boltshauser/Kuvien Images

Directions

a. Transfer processed cake and cookie crumbs to a large bowl.
b. Combine water, cocoa and sugar in a pot. Bring to a boil, mixing until it thickens enough to coat the back of a spoon. Remove from heat.
c. Immediately add the margarine and vanilla. Mix until margarine completely dissolves.
d. Add Liquor.
e. Set aside half of the glaze. Pour the other half of the glaze mixture over the reserved cake crumbs in the large bowl. Mix well and let cool.
f. For the assembly:

⇨ Cut the sponge cake in half horizontally.

⇨ Spread the glaze (that was set aside) between the two layers of sponge cake, leaving enough of the mixture to smear on top of cake, if desired.

Using the crumb glaze mixture, form a disk by hand, about one inch thick, the same diameter as the sponge cake, and place it over one layer of the cake which is used as the base.
  Slide or carefully place the cake on top of the crumb mixture base.

⇨ Spread the top of the cake with the remaining glaze. Garnish with sprinkles on top of glaze.

RUM BALLS

Ingredients

4 Cups Assorted leftover cake (Cream cakes are fine)
2 heaping Tbsp. Cocoa
10 Tbsp. Water (⅔ Cup *minus* 2 tsps.)
4 Tbsp. Sugar
1 tsp. Vanilla
3 Tbsp. Sherry or other liqueur (optional)
½ stick (¼ Cup) Margarine

Directions

a. Crumble leftover cake. (If you have doughy cake like kokosh, use a food processor to crumble it.) Set aside in a large bowl.
b. Combine cocoa, water and sugar in a pot. Mix very well.
c. Cook the cocoa mixture mixing constantly until it thickens and coats the back of the spoon. Add the margarine, mix until it dissolves. Remove from heat.
d. Add vanilla and let cool.
e. Add sherry.
f. Pour the mixture on top of the cake crumbs, mix. Form firm balls. You can roll the balls in colorful or plain sugar, sprinkles or coconut.

janosmarton/Shutterstock.com

SHAPE-A-CAKE

You can create shaped cakes using the crumb mixture described above (Cake Crumbs). Double or triple the amount according to need. Here are directions for a doll cake, a house cake, a lady and a man's hat cake. If you can create shapes from play dough you can use this talent to create animals or large balls from this cake mixture and cover with cream. The sky is the limit.

Doll Cake

Shape the crumbs mixture into a cone.
Stick a Barbie doll into the cone. The waist of the doll should be sticking out above the cone. Cover the cone and the doll's torso with cream to create a dress or gown.

House-Shape Cake

Shape the mixture into a small box. Cover the whole cake with cream. Colorful candies can be used as a door shape and window shape.
Add wafers for a roof.
Cover with cream and decorate the roof with red candies.

Lady's Hat Cake

These were prepared for an engagement party.

Cut a flat cardboard into a circle 2 inches larger than the diameter of the cake. Place the cake on the cardboard and cover the cake and cardboard with white fondant. Smooth it out. Put some ribbons around the cake. It will look like a lady's hat.

TRIFLE

You will need a tall glass trifle dish for this recipe.

Ingredients

3 Cups Assorted pieces of leftover cake. (*Not* doughy cake.)
1 Container *Parev* whipping cream (8 ounces)
½ Cup Sugar
5–6 Tbsp. Liquor or wine
Chocolate curls or plain grated

Directions

a. Whip the cream and sugar, until stiff.
b. Line the bottom of the trifle dish with 1 cup of cake pieces.
c. Sprinkle liquor or wine on top.
d. Spread about 1cup of whipped cream on top.

e. Repeat, ending with the whipped cream.

f. Sprinkle with chocolate curls on top.

Tip: The layers should be as neat as possible. When assembling the trifle, keep checking how it looks from the outside of the glass bowl.

zefirchik06/Shutterstock.com

⇨ *Variation 1:* Add a layer of strawberries or blueberries. Add crushed walnuts or pieces of leftover dried fruits cut into small pieces.

⇨ *Variation 2:* The same layers can be placed in individual tall glasses.

LESSON 8

MANAGING YOUR PANTRY AND GENERAL TIPS

Managing Your Pantry

Having a well-stocked pantry can help you reinvent your leftovers. If you just have one or two portions, consider eating the leftovers "as is" or adding just one or two ingredients. For a large pot of leftovers, one has to be creative. I try to use leftovers as soon as possible or to freeze them.

General suggestions for using leftovers:

- Reheat with additional ingredients

- Make sandwiches

- Add to another dish

- Cook in a new way

- Freeze for later

- For all staples that you use regularly in your kitchen, always have one open bag and one back up, right behind it. For example, one open bag of flour and a closed one behind it. As soon as the open bag is finished, add it to your grocery list. Have a system of placing the newer items behind the older ones to make sure that you reach for the older ones first. This applies to other foods such as ketchup, mayonnaise, mustard, soy sauce, etc.

- Items with shorter shelf lives can be kept in the refrigerator, such as flour, bread crumbs, even cereals. I use only dry yeast and keep it in the freezer for months.

✍ Keep items in your pantry that do *not* perish easily.
For example, corn syrup, powdered sugar, dried fruits, chocolate or cocoa, and other ingredients that you may not need frequently but you can always count on having to cook or bake without having to rush out to the grocery. Added to this list are vanilla, vanilla sugar and most canned goods. It is good to have a variety. A tasty side dish can be prepared in minutes with a mix of canned vegetables, such as corn, green beans, mushrooms, and peas with some salt, garlic powder, and black pepper, drizzled with oil and served.

✍ Spices are best stored in the freezer. When you want to try out a new spice try to buy the smallest container possible, because you don't know how you or your family will like it. It shouldn't go to waste if you do not like it.

✍ In order to use this book most efficiently, have freezer items available, such as wraps, frozen mini *bourekas*, piecrusts and other items that you can use for leftovers.

✍ Make a note from Chanukah until Pesach, to use up *chametz* items in your pantry. For example, don't stock up on noodles at this time of year. With careful planning, you will eliminate the big waste of throwing out good food and nosh before the holiday.

General Tips

Before we conclude I would like to share some final tips with you.

1. Using Ingredients Before they Spoil

🖋 When you have an open can of tomato paste, for example, don't leave it in the back of the refrigerator until it spoils. It can be used in a soup or in a stew. It can be mixed with some water instead of tomato sauce or in a blender with some other vegetables, instead of tomato juice or ketchup.

🖋 Extra wine can be used in a roast or mix with seltzer for a fancy drink. White dry wine can be used in some recipes that call for vinegar.

🖋 At the end of the summer we are often left with open bottles of sauces which were used for barbeques. Don't keep them in the back of the refrigerator until Pesach when it must be thrown out. *Use it up table-spoon by tablespoon.* A little in the vegetable soup, some on a roast, some in the *cholent* or in one of the cooked vegetables. The same goes for many other ingredients such as mustard, fruits, vegetables and spices.

(One time I had cooked up too much apple sauce. I added some eggs, a few tablespoons of flour, poured it into a pie crust, baked it at 350° F for about an hour and was rewarded with a delicious apple pie.)

2. Presenting New Foods to Children

🖊 Encourage your family members to refrain from vocalizing any negative comments – if they don't like it, they don't have to eat it, but they shouldn't say anything negative about the food presented (especially not "yuck!"). Let the young ones form their own opinions. Young children are often willing to try new things.

🖊 Serve the new food as the first course, when they are the hungriest.

🖊 Repeat giving the new food and show them how you and others in the family enjoy it.

🖊 Parents can enjoy a new dish in front of the children that is presented "only for Mommy and Daddy to eat." I guarantee that after seeing the parents enjoying a new food this way once or twice, the kids will soon ask for it too.

3. Using Substitutes

There are many food products available today that can be *parev* substitutes for milk, cheese and yogurt. Similarly, other ingredients can easily be substituted, such as when a recipe calls for wine in baking, a ½ cup of water mixed with ½ cup of vinegar serves well. Lemonade and orange juice can be interchanged, as can rice and orzo. The possibilities are limited only by our own creativity.

4. Using Liquids

By liquids I am referring to the liquids that the vegetables, meats, and chicken were cooking in.

🖊 Clear, strained liquid from cooked vegetables can be used in chicken soup when you start to cook or even added once the soup is ready.

🖊 If the liquid is cloudy, for example when you cook potatoes, it can be used in a vegetable soup.

Many liquids can be enjoyed as is, a vegetable tea of sorts, delicious and nutritious. The liquid left after cooking beets is excellent.

Liquids left after cooking fruits can be served as fruit punch.

My grandchildren know that in Grandma's house they can have fresh apple juice. (The liquid strained from cooking apples.)

A woman was telling me that she discards any liquid left in the pan after baking chicken or a roast. Those flavorful liquids should *never* be thrown away. I pour off liquids into a jar, refrigerate it overnight, and the next day I remove the fat accumulated at the top. This liquid can then be used to enrich soups or cooked vegetables and *cholent*. *Delicious*!

5. Spices

Notice that in most recipes in this book I use basic spices – salt, pepper, and garlic powder. You are welcome to experiment with other spices however you can produce delicious dishes with these spices, on their own.

If you're looking to cut back on salt, reduce the amount of processed foods in your diet. This is the salt that causes the most harm. Adding a controlled amount of salt in your own home-cooking is fine and will enhance the flavor of your dishes.

6. Fire, Heat and Safety

Be vigilant and diligent especially when frying.

Handles of cookware should be turned towards the back to avoid accidental splashes or spills.

When frying, make sure children are not running around near you.

Always have baking soda or a fire extinguisher nearby.

When finished using the hand immersion blender, disconnect it from the electricity right away. My dear friend Chavi hurt herself very badly when she started to clean the hand blender while it was still plugged in!

If G-d forbid a frying pan catches on fire, first shut the fire or electricity (if it is an electric burner); then cover the frying pan with a metal cover. (If the fire is out of control, make sure everyone in the house gets out, and then call the fire department.)

7. General Tips to Use in the Kitchen

While cleanliness is paramount in the kitchen, there are some shortcuts that can save you time. Before starting your cooking, clear the counters and wipe them down. Put away dishes and items that you are not using. While cooking or baking, save washing for the very end.

When measuring flour into a cup , rest the cup in a sink so that any extra flour will fall in the sink for an easier cleanup.

Always use a larger pot then needed. For anything you cook, you should use a bigger pot then the amount of food calls for. The reasoning is that the food will have room to cook, you will have room to turn and mix the food without spilling onto the stove, and when you wash up, the size of the pot does not add that much work.

When a recipe says "salt and pepper to taste" your job is to actually taste the food and correct the seasoning.

Arrange your pots and pans so that frequently used ones are in the front. Store large pots on higher shelves or in higher cabinets. Avoid having small items on high shelves.

8. Creating Your Own Recipes

When using leftovers to create your own recipes, first take an inventory of the foods you have, then pair them up with other ingredients on hand, add herbs and seasonings and in no time you will have created tasty dishes to share with your family. Here are some quick and easy ideas.

If you have some *not so fresh* vegetables at home, you can put them in a pot, cover with water, cook for a while, add seasoning, and you have a soup. You can use an immersion blender, taste and adjust the seasoning, and it's ready to serve. No recipe needed.

If you have cooked vegetables, you can add a few eggs, a few tablespoons of flour, (approximately one egg and one tablespoon of flour for every Cupful of cooked vegetable), seasoning, place in the oven on 350° F for an hour, and voila! You have a delicious kugel.

Another use for cooked vegetables, is to make a frittata by adding 3 eggs and seasoning for every cup of mashed vegetables, and frying the mixture in a frying pan on a low heat until the top is firm. *Unbelievably delicious*!

Vegetable soups can be a new creation every time you cook one. Each batch is made from vegetables that you have on hand. To that, you have the option of adding tomato sauce, noodles, beans, and so on. You can cut the vegetables into small pieces or leave them whole, cook for a while, and cut them when they are soft. You can add some mashed potato or some flour to thicken the soup as well.

The next time you read a recipe, try to imagine the tastes each ingredient will bring into the dish. You can develop this sense over time.

Baking tends to require stricter adherence to a recipe then cooking does. The amounts of each ingredient as well as the combination of ingredients is important. However, even with baking, some experimenting can prove successful.

Substituting oil for margarine in cake recipes is one such option.

The amount of sugar in many cakes can be reduced by a quarter of a cup at a time, until you determine the right balance in the end product.

An extra egg can be added to most cake recipes for extra fluffiness.

The general idea is to enjoy what you are doing, be willing to experiment and be creative. Most importantly, imagine how a certain ingredient will alter the cake or dish you are working on.

Your own satisfaction and pleasure upon discovering a new twist on a recipe is immeasurable.

The same applies to decorating and presenting your food.

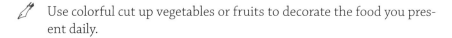 Use colorful cut up vegetables or fruits to decorate the food you present daily.

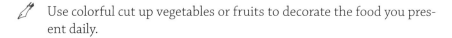 Work simple designs into your food using a knife or tablespoon, for example, creating waves on mashed potatoes, and you will easily create an impressive presentation that is memorable for your family and guests.

9. What to do with a Burnt Dish

A burnt dish need not necessarily be sent straight to the garbage. First assess the damage.

A pot on the stove can be checked for the extent of the burned food with a flat spatula. If you can scrape it up easily and the burnt part is brown (not black), you can mix it in, and believe it or not, it will give the dish a good taste. If the bottom is black, however, and cannot be scraped up easily, try to save as much as you can from above the burnt part, and discard the rest. If what you saved has a burnt taste discard the whole dish.

If the dish is still raw, transfer to another pot and finish cooking. Be extra careful with bean dishes, making sure you keep mixing the contents of the pot in order to avoid burning, since beans, in particular, can absorb the burnt taste faster than other dishes. We proceed with cakes the same way. First check what the damage is and see which part can be saved and how it might be used in a different way. Try my suggestions for cake crumbs. (See Section II: Tasty Desserts in Lesson 7 Challah, Bread & Cake.)

I must share my own mishap, as we all have such experiences. I had peeled, cored and cut apples for apple sauce and prepared four 9" × 13" pans. I set the temperature on 400° F and planned to shut it off after an hour. I didn't put on a timer (my first mistake) and went up to lay down. Four hours later I woke up to smell my disaster! These things happen but after mourning the loss of money, time and effort, we move on, hopefully learning from our mistakes.

Closing Thoughts

My dear friends we have arrived at the last page. I hope you have learned some new concepts and will implement them in your own cooking.

My personal mission for this book is learning how to use leftovers in a new and creative way, and above all, enjoying the sense of satisfaction in doing so.

Remember that you don't have to stick religiously to a recipe. You can modify it by adding ingredients, substituting other ingredients, or leaving out some ingredients. The possibilities are endless.

I recently heard about a daughter who asked her mother "Why didn't we ever have leftovers in our home?" and the mother answered simply, "We *did* have leftovers but I always presented it the next day in a different way." If we can reach such a stage where our family doesn't realize that they are having leftovers, we can pat ourselves on the back.

Good luck and keep in touch. I will try my best to answer questions. I welcome comments and suggestions as well. I will be happy to receive ideas for my next book!

My e-mail is SUNSHINEHOMES18@gmail.com.

List of Recipes

Index
